REJECTION EXPOSED

UNDERSTANDING THE ROOT AND FRUIT OF REJECTION

ANTHONY HULSEBUS

ACKNOWLEDGEMENTS

FIRST AND FOREMOST I WANT TO ACKNOWLEDGE and thank my awesome wife, Susan, who has always believed in me and the ministry God has given me. I am especially grateful for her constant encouragement to "go and write." She always gave me the grace and space to write what God has put in my heart. I also want to thank Zoe and Zachary, our two gifts from God, who had to put up with my strange hours and absence when in my writing moods and who have taught me about unconditional love.

In addition I want to acknowledge the monthly partners of Dominion Ministries without whose prayers and support this book would not have been possible. It is through their faithfulness that I had the time to write this book and will write many others that I humbly pray will bless many, many lives.

Susan and I thank all those who have prayed for us, supported us, and believed in us in the early years of our ministry.

Finally, many thanks to David Sluka whose patience and wisdom helped me arrive at this end product.

CONTENTS

Introduction 7

Chapter 1: Discerning the Root.....................................9

Chapter 2: Exposing the Real Enemy............................27

Chapter 3: Rejection and Spiritual Warfare 51

Chapter 4: Rejection and Rebellion 75

Chapter 5: Rejection and Self-Pity................................89

Chapter 6: Rejection and the Fear of Man...................107

Chapter 7: Passive Rejection 121

Chapter 8: The Seven Deadly Fruits of Rejection 135

Chapter 9: W.D.D.D.—What Did David Do? 147

Chapter 10: W.D.I.D.—What do I Do?........................159

Chapter 11: You Can Do This!.....................................183

Chapter 12: Confession and Freedom...........................189

Endnotes 207

INTRODUCTION

Since the first printing of this book, I have realized that some people do not feel they have an issue with rejection because they do not exhibit some of the signs that indicate the presence of a spirit of rejection.

Yet in further discussion, we discover that indeed they do struggle with the roots of rejection but it was hidden from them. So even if you don't fit what you might consider a classic rejected personal profile, I want to encourage you to glean whatever you can from this book. Even a little bit of unhealed rejection can cause major relational issues with God and those around you. I believe there is a reason you have this book in your hands and I trust you will keep an open mind as your read.

My wife, Susan, and I have found over years of ministry that rejection is the "strongman" that Jesus speaks of in Mark 3:27—in other words, the root cause of our struggles. But we have also found that most people's strongman hides from them. And why not? The apostle Paul told Timothy that "we are not ignorant of his [the devil's] schemes" (1 Timothy 2:23). Demons scheme against humanity and they hide their main work against us. If you are not comfortable with the concept of demons, chapter 3 will help you to understand that we are in a very real spiritual battle, and what you don't know *can* hurt you.

Everyone has experienced different levels of rejection, and rejection damages each person uniquely. Wherever you are in your walk in relation to rejection issues in your life, I know through experience that the truths contained in this book will set you free!

CHAPTER 1

DISCERNING THE ROOT

A long, long time ago in a lush garden, a beautiful and innocent young woman lay out in the warm afternoon sunshine by herself. As she lay there half asleep, she heard a voice behind her. It was a strange voice that piqued her curiosity. She turned and saw a familiar, handsome creature speaking to her. The creature began to say things about the woman's lover—challenging things, things she didn't like to hear. It told her that her lover had lied to her, that he was holding out on her, and had not been fully honest.

As the women listened, she became more and more angry, feeling betrayed and completely rejected. And though she tried to defend her lover to the creature, it was no use. His onslaught was subtle yet powerful. Finally, the young women decided to get even. She rebelled against her lover and did the very thing he had warned would cost her the life he had given her. Her rejection led to her rebellion.

Do you recognize these events? They took place in the Garden of Eden. The beautiful, young woman was Eve—the mother of the living.

The stranger was satan and her lover was God Himself. The deed of retaliation? It involved a piece of fruit, but the root was rejection.

Roots and Fruits

If there is one thing we all can agree on, it's this: bad things happen in life. Just read the paper, open your e-mail, surf the Web, or watch the evening news. We all get hurt and we all hurt others. We're part victims and part villains, so we all have pain and "issues" in our lives. But the question remains, *what do we do about it?* I suggest we have missed the answer in two areas: first, we have focused on the *fruit* and not the *root*, and second, we have ignored the spiritual side of life.

Many of us struggle with the *fruits* of anger, fear, anxiety, addictions, lust, lying, cheating, stealing, depression, etc. We don't like the bad fruit in our lives (or in the lives of others) and we all try to fix it in many ways. We try better or different friends, new hobbies, new clothes, new jobs, new location, therapy, and even religion, but we often don't experience the change we want. We have failed to see the *root* of the problem, so we can never change the *fruit*. Our issues become the proverbial weed in the sidewalk that we pull every week, but it just keeps growing back because we can't get at the root! We constantly ask ourselves, *"What is my problem?"* or *"What is their problem?"*

If that is you or someone you love, I have great news for you. This book can go a long way in breaking that cycle and setting you and them free. And here's the really good news—it's not complicated, because the root is based in one simple but powerful word—*rejection*. This is mankind's universal problem. Mankind generally lives rejected, with a deep-rooted sense of failure and/or disappointment—what I call a *root of rejection.*

Rejection is also our greatest fear. We take amazing steps—some of them not so healthy—to be accepted and avoid rejection. We fear rejection like a person who just whacked their thumb with a hammer would fear a handshake. When we are "throbbing with pain" on the inside, we avoid anything that smells like rejection.

Now, without giving a lesson in agriculture here, let's look at some definitions of *root* and *fruit*. Merriam-Webster's Collegiate Dictionary defines *root* as "something that is an origin or source" and "the essential core, heart."[1] Plainly stated, the root is the origin or cause of any thing.

Fruit has an obvious definition, but I summarize it this way: *fruit* is what comes from what is planted. Jesus said it this way:

> "So every good tree bears good fruit, but the bad tree bears bad fruit. A good tree cannot produce bad fruit, nor can a bad tree produce good fruit…So then, you will know them by their fruits." —Matthew 7:17–20

We also know that the fruit that we are seeking is not literal, but spiritual and eternal, as this verse points out:

> Woe to those who are heroes at drinking wine…their **root** will rot and their blossom [*fruit*] will blow away as dust, for they have rejected the law of the Lord. —Isaiah 5:22, 24

Note that Isaiah doesn't say that those who have rotten roots will simply produce fruit that is of no value. He says that they are blown away as dust! See these other biblical references:

> See to it that no one fails to obtain the grace of God; that no root of bitterness springs up and causes trouble, and by it many become defiled. —Hebrews 12:15

If we can have a root of bitterness, we can also have a root of rejection. Rejection and bitterness are conditions of our hearts. Hebrews says that bitterness can defile many. I would say rejection does the same. While it mostly defiles the one with the rejection, it will also defile others. It pollutes, perverts, and strains almost all relationships.

"…and they have **no root in themselves**, and so endure only
for a time. Afterward, when tribulation or persecution arises
for the word's sake, immediately they stumble."
—Mark 4:17, NKJV

Jesus here states that those who stop following Him because of persecution and trials have no root in themselves. The point here is that the root speaks to our baseline of strength of character, foundation, and health of our spirit or heart. We all have a root or baseline from which we live. Remember a root is what feeds us, just like a root feeds a plant. But most have either an infected root or one so damaged that it's as if we had no root at all—no stability or foundation to hold us on course.

I recently had a root canal, which I don't recommend, but I learned about dead and dying roots. In our teeth, the nerves and their roots can be dead or decaying and thus cause us much pain! That can be a picture of you and me. We have roots that, through rejection, are dead or dying, but God can come with His love and affirmation and heal our roots and even give us new ones! No dentist can do that!

Since rejection is a *spiritual*, eternal force (as is love), when it is sown in our hearts as a seed through words and actions against us, it produces a *spiritual* root. Just like when I plant a sunflower seed in the soil, it germinates, sprouts a root, and, small though it starts, produces a giant stalk of a sunflower, which then produces many other seeds. So it is with spiritual things, whether for good or evil.

Now the question is, if one has had rejection "planted" in their heart and it has become the root of their life, what is the fruit? That is the essence of this book—identifying the fruit and its source, which for most of us, is rejection. We then want to help you have a new root, which is the love of God.

There are only two roots in life—acceptance or rejection. Either God has accepted you or He has rejected you. You're either in the family of

God or out. You're either a son or daughter of God or you're not. Most don't like it said that simply, but it can be no other way.

Since rejection is universal and there is no one who escapes some level of rejection, the question is not if you will be rejected, but what will you do when it comes your way. Therapists have other names for your emotional woes. Commonly they would say it is *low self-esteem*. But I have zeroed in on rejection because it's the initial act or action that causes low self-esteem. In other words, low self-esteem is a fruit. Rejection is the root. You will never remove a root by treating the fruit, but you will change the fruit in your life by changing the roots that feed your internal life.

So, roots do two things. First, they *feed us* from what they are made of or are tapped into. Second, they *hold truth or lies*, which determine the health of our "plant" or heart. A rejected root is weak and sick. An accepted, loved root is strong and healthy. Which root do you have?

Once you know why you are carrying the burdens, pains, sorrows, and sadness that you do, you will be much more likely to be free. My wife, Susan, and I have had many people come to us over the years who say, "I feel ___ (sad, mad, pained, depressed, etc.) and I don't know why." We then help them discover the why and then equip them to learn how this thing called rejection works. But the main thing people fail to realize is the spiritual side of rejection, and really, of life itself.

The Spirit in Life

Statistically, 92 percent of Americans believe in God, and at least 50 percent say they pray on a daily basis.[2] I can imagine that if you have picked up this book, you have prayed in some manner for help with your issues. So I also assume you will be open to the idea that the answer to your struggles in life could be a spiritual one, at least in part. The truth is that you and I are spirits who live in a body. We are spiritual beings. As you read this book, I simply ask you to be open to the spiritual aspect of your struggles and the possibility that there is more to this life than meets your physical eye.

I would guess that anyone who had been to a funeral and looked at a loved one in a coffin has wondered what happens when we die. *Is this all there is? What happened to Uncle Bob? One minute we're alive and then where is that life?* That "life" that is in those who walk on this earth is what the Bible calls "the spirit of man." In the book of Job, it says:

> It is the spirit of man, the breath of the Almighty, that gives him [man] understanding. —Job 32:8

Every major religion embraces an afterlife and the eternal existence of the spirit, but we need to know just exactly how the spirit realm affects us today in our emotions and our bodies. Even Hollywood is producing shows about angels, mediums, psychics, and demons. Yet if a Christian preacher mentions these things, we tend to balk. Why do we trust Hollywood more than the Bible? It's a matter of exposure. You have most likely seen way more of Hollywood than you have read the Bible. But here's the funny part: when it comes to one aspect of the Bible, Hollywood is in some level of agreement with it. There *are* demons and angels (though the angels from Hollywood are nothing like the real ones, and neither are the demons) and they do interact with us on a daily basis, either for good or for evil.

I am inviting you to explore with me the spiritual side of rejection and its affects. If you will keep an open mind regarding this aspect of life, whether you are a Christian or not, the Biblical principles we look at will help you as they have helped many, many others. This book is not designed to convert the non-Christian, but to help the hurting of all backgrounds recover from the effects of rejection. It's been my experience that the Bible gives us the best example of those who have endured tremendous amounts of personal pain and how they handled it—some well and some not so well. God gives us a glimpse into the personal lives of some great men and women, and also some not-so-great men and women. Through it all, the common thread is that they endured much rejection at the hands of loved ones, fellow countrymen, and their enemies.

I truly believe, as someone who has endured a lot of rejection personally, that what I am sharing from years of prayer, counseling, personal experience, research, and study will help you. While I am not a professional counselor, therapist, or psychologist, I have for many years, as a minister, prayed with thousands of people all over the world whose lives have been truly damaged by rejection. By applying the principles of this book, I have seen many greatly helped and set free from the effects of rejection.

In this book, we'll discover how rejection works, what it leads to in our lives, and how we can defeat it once and for all. No one is exempt from rejection, so we will continue to experience it, but we don't all respond to it the same. There are different forms and degrees of rejection. Even if you haven't dealt with it in the past, you will encounter some level of rejection in the future. What I have learned is that most people dismiss the effects of rejection in their life. They have had to in order to survive. But that doesn't mean the effect is not there; it just means it's buried. It's buried in memories and those memories are still alive, even if they are compartmentalized to help us cope with life. Jesus said of Himself, "I came to heal the brokenhearted [lit. Hebrew—shattered minds]" (Isaiah 61:1). Your broken heart or shattered mind can be healed.

> Most people dismiss the effects of rejection in their life. They have had to in order to survive.

Rejection and Its Fruit

I separate rejection into two general categories: passive and active. Then I categorize four general reactions to rejection:

- Doubt and fear—doubt that we are loved and fear that we are not lovable and will never be loved, often leading to anxiety.
- Anger—at the rejecter, God, authority, and ourselves, which leads us to reject others.
- Withdrawal and self-pity—a personal shutdown to meaningful relationships, often leading to depression.
- Denial—the "happy cover-up," smiling on the outside, crying on the inside, often leading to isolation and loneliness.

Of course not all rejection leaves us neatly in just one of these categories. Normally, there is a mixture of two or more responses to rejection in our lives, or even all four, as we pass through stages of self-realization.

Perhaps you're thinking this is just a rough spot in your life and you'll be fine with more prayer, more church time, a new job, new friends, etc. Perhaps you may still wonder if rejection is really that big of a deal. Well, it is.

One of the most successful, famous, and wealthiest people in our modern times was the late pop icon Michael Jackson. In a recent interview, his friend Rabbi Shmuley Boteach said:

> I'm speaking specifically as the years went on, I think Michael lived with a profound fear of rejection. And Michael told me once—and this is a heartbreaking conversation between us—"Shmuley, I promise I'm not lying to you," he said. "I'm not lying to you." He said that twice. "But everything I've done in pursuing fame, in honing my craft," to quote his words, "was an effort to be loved, because I never felt loved." And he used to say that to me all the time…he said that he lived for his father's approval.[3]

Never underestimate the power of rejection, especially from a father. I have spent years counseling people who have become relationally dysfunctional with both God and others because of rejection. It has greatly affected my life in almost every area, but especially in my relationship with God and my family.

Your relationship with your father will establish, in large part, how you perceive God and how you will relate to Him the rest of your life, for better or for worse. Whether it is passive rejection (indifference) or active rejection (such as verbal, physical, or sexual abuse), rejection from a father is the number one issue that I address in my counseling sessions. Secular research has confirmed over and over the power of the father's influence.

> It's not that rejection is so powerful in and of itself, but rather it's that *our need for love and acceptance is so strong* that it amplifies the effects of rejection.

Today, in America anyway, we live in the most fatherless generation in history. So even if it's passive rejection (absent father), it's still rejection. Now, that is not to say that some of you reading this book have not suffered greatly because of rejection from your mother, for we know that can also be very painful. But I have seen deeper and more numerous wounds resulting from a father's rejection than from a mother's.

Again, one could pause and ask, "Why do these instances of rejection affect me so much?" I would state the answer like this: It's not that rejection is so powerful in and of itself, but rather it's that *our need for love and acceptance is so strong* that it amplifies the effects of rejection.

Read the above statement again—it's important! You see, God made us deficient, if you will. Without true unconditional love, we're like tires without air, trees without leaves, or a car without an engine. We are all just an empty shell without the spiritual force of love filling us up. We are needy and empty by design. Some people never recognize this and so they either despise the idea that they need anyone (especially God) or believe their efforts to get love, even when sinful, are normal. But because of the rejection in their lives, many people know that they are still empty, lonely, sad, and depressed. Some people mask the effects of rejection with overly outgoing behavior, talking too much, or keeping too busy, hoping that the unwanted feelings will go away. Of course they don't go away; they just hide. I've learned this much over the years: your rejection will come out; it just depends how.

There are many, many different coping mechanisms for rejection, but they have one thing in common: they want to avoid pain. What research, the Bible, and my personal experience have taught me is that the memories of the rejections—which are spiritual, emotional, and physical—don't go away like water down a drain, even though they can diminish with time to some degree. Rather, they need to be healed. Jesus said He came to "*heal* the broken hearted." So for every rejection, there must be a healing of some level.

The great scientist Sir Isaac Newton demonstrated that each action has an equal and opposite reaction. The power of rejection should never be underestimated. It is, in fact, an equal and yet opposite force to love. And we all know how powerful love is in our lives and in the lives of others.

Give and Take

As I implied from Newton's law of reciprocal action, love and rejection act the same. I might say it this way:

> For each and every rejection, there must be an act of love, whether verbal, physical, or emotional, to replace and remake what rejection has stolen.

Yes, I mean *stolen*, for I have learned that rejection does steal. Make no mistake, rejection and the memories imbedded in us keep on stealing from us even after the initial event, because we not only experience the initial rejection, but we carry the memory of rejection until it is healed. Modern neuroscience has proven that rejection is even carried in the physical cells of our body. So rejection continues to steal from us in many ways years after the event. Most of us can remember painful moments for a lifetime. But, by God's grace, the memory *can* lose its painful power.

What rejection steals the most from you is your God-given identity. What I mean is that it tells you that you are something you are not or something that God didn't make you to be. Or rejection tells you that you are something that is bad—you're a failure, you're stupid, etc. The "voice" of rejection speaks to your heart because it has at its root a spiritual force behind it, even if that voice comes through people who are close to you.

> What rejection steals the most from you is your God-given identity.

If you don't know who God made you to be, or what I call your "kingdom (of God) identity," you will only assume the identity you learned from your childhood or your environment. Thus you will always feel somewhat lost in certain areas of your life. It will make you feel like you always have a broken piece to what I call your "identity mirror."

I am not talking about your physical identity, but rather your *heart identity*. It works like this. When you think about yourself, regardless of whether you like yourself or if others like or love you, what do you see? What you *see* in your heart about yourself is how you *feel* in your heart about yourself. And how you *feel* is how you *act*, and how you *act* determines how others *treat* you, and that oftentimes determines the level of joy of your life.

Remember those funny mirrors at amusement parks or state fairs? You know, the ones that make you look really short or tall, fat or skinny, or really wavy and weird? That is what rejection does to your self-image/

God-image. It perverts it, makes it out of shape and abnormal, so when you look into your heart, you see things you don't like. (I know I never looked good in those mirrors!) You "see" the words spoken over you or the physical abuses you may have endured in life. These things all told you lies about who you are and when you believed them, your image became warped. Your identity mirror was bent and now you can't see whom God made you to be, which causes confusion, frustration, and a whole host of pain in our lives.

Another way to think of rejection is like you would your bank account. Each instance of rejection is a withdrawal on your account, whereas an act of love, affection, or affirmation is a deposit. It doesn't take long to see why we start feeling spiritually and emotionally overdrawn. Being overdrawn can make us do bad things, just as poor people who become financially desperate steal because they think they have no alternative. In the same way, we hurt others, especially God, when we believe we are poor in love and overdrawn emotionally. In fact, it is a truth to say that rejected people reject others and the more rejected one is, the more he or she rejects those around them, especially loved ones.

When humans feel emotionally poor, they will always overcompensate to correct it. Sadly, we often accept a human substitute for what only God's love can heal. On the other hand, if someone is full of God's love, human rejection will have little to no effect. I am writing from the perspective that we exist primarily for God and thus, we, without a relationship with God, will always be emotionally deficient. It is our task in life to find the love that God has to offer and thus become secure in the battles that life on earth can bring.

What Rejection Is and Is Not

Before we get into this too deep, it might be helpful to define what rejection is and what it is not. First, real rejection is *not* when you don't get your way. While you may feel rejected and thus mad or sad, I do not count this as rejection. If you desire something (or someone) and it is neither God's best nor His plan for you, or if your motive is selfish and impure, then not getting your way may have been the very best thing. The "no" that you dislike is not rejection, even though it feels that way. We must know that if we don't discern true rejection from false rejection, we may end up taking far too many things as personal rejection and thus develop a mindset or lifestyle of expecting rejection even before it happens. If we do this, it creates a bitter, critical, or shameful heart that no one wants to be around, which invites even more real rejection!

Someone may, from loving intentions, deny your desire and yet you feel rejected. For instance, if my son wants a second cookie after dinner and I say no, I am, in fact, not rejecting him, but protecting him. Ah, but you may say he *felt* rejected, rebuffed, and wronged by his cruel and controlling father! Yes, all that may be true, but we have to distinguish between *real* rejection and *felt* rejection to know *how* to deal with it and find the *real* cure.

Real rejection in this cookie scenario may happen if I have *promised* a cookie to my son, *but* at the last minute I say, "No, you can't have a cookie, you little ankle-biter," or some such terrible thing. Here I have wrongly accused him, denied him something I promised, and threw in a dose of shame to boot! There is no miscommunication here, no selfish desire, but simply a broken promise with some name-calling thrown in. My son would feel rejected and rightly so.

> If we go to God at the moment of feeling rejected and ask Him to help, we can find out the truth of the hurt.

So how do we determine true and false feelings of rejection? Well, you can't, not at first, because the emotions run strong and overshadow reason. But if we go to God at the moment of feeling rejected and ask Him to help, we can find out the truth of the hurt.

Whether we had wrong desires, missed God's will, miscommunicated, or were miscommunicated with, we're still hurt, right? But when the situation is looked into, whether five minutes or fifty years later, we must examine the scenario and *our hearts* as best we can and deal with the situation accordingly. One situation may call for forgiveness while another may call for us to repent for our own actions that caused the *perceived* rejection from the other party.

Rejection Defined

So what is rejection? Here is my definition: When you are *wrongly* hurt by *words, actions,* and/or *indifference* to the point of embracing *personal pain* and *believing a lie* about your true, God-given *identity.*

I italicized key concepts above in my definition and will cover these areas repeatedly in this book. But let's just string them together: wrongly, words, actions, indifference, personal pain, believing a lie, and identity. Each of these keywords plays a part in how you and I experience and respond to rejection. I emphasize *wrongly* because there are times that we are rejected, or least certainly feel rejected, but are actually just not getting what we want. So much of our culture demands instant gratification that for some to be denied their desires feels like real rejection. If you miss this distinction, you will fail to properly deal with real rejection.

The other concept missed so often is how rejection tries to change your identity. This is the most forgotten and yet most damaging aspect of rejection. We see in the above definition that rejection can be actions and/or indifference, which is why we break rejection down into two categories:

- Active Rejection—intentional or planned actions carried out in spoken words and/or physical actions against us.
- Passive Rejection—the indifference of or general neglect from someone who is designed to give you love, affirmation,

and affection, normally a parent, spouse, friend, or someone else important in your life.

Now most people would say that active rejection is the most painful, but research and experience does not back this up. God has designed the family, the church, and society in general to have certain relationships that are meant to prepare us to receive His love and affirmation, creating the ability for us to relate to the ultimate source of love—God Himself. The family is the first place for this, so parents were meant to create an image inside of you of someone who is worthy of receiving and giving love. When you do not experience the love and affirmation of a parent, especially that of your father, you will immediately have a breakdown of your ability to function in life.

Think of bread with no yeast; it never rises to its potential, but instead ends up hard, flat, and tasteless. You were actually so strongly designed to receive love that even *passive* rejection of a parent can greatly damage you.

> Though we don't always react to rejection the same, the good news is that the solution is simple and always the same!

Many therapists would point out that patients who endured physical, verbal, and even sexual abuse from parents have told them that at least these acts gave them some level of attention. While that seems warped and even sick, in stands in contrast to the children who never got the time of day from or never knew their parents. Research shows that parents who completely neglect their children can hurt them just as badly as those who abuse their children.

The danger of categories and labels as it relates to someone's personal life is that it can cause us to think we're just a statistic or a number or part of a common trend that diminishes our uniqueness. But let me say that though we don't always react to rejection the same, the good news is that the solution is simple and always the same! Perhaps you have tried many methods and counselors to get free from your pain and, at this point, are not too hopeful. I understand, as it took many years for me to understand and get healing from my rejection, and I am not finished. But I have seen a much faster process for those we've worked with by applying the truths God has showed me over many years. I hope to shorten your process by helping you learn from my mistakes. So no matter what cycle or phase you are in and no matter what you have experienced, there is hope for healing and wholeness in the principles laid out in this book. The timetable will be different for each person to realize full healing, but the solution is the same.

Since the Bible is the best book I have found with the most honest and open account of people's lives, I am using the personal case studies therein to point out the effects of, and process of healing from, rejection (I am glad I was not written about in the Bible). Whether or not you are a Christian, the Bible has been the most trusted book on moral and spiritual truths since the time is was written. I ask you to keep an open heart in regards to its message.

At the end of each chapter I provide questions for you personally or for group study that will help you reflect and grow from what was presented. But the best path to healing is to use the separate workbooks for both of our books on rejection as they are much more detailed and have many insightful questions that help you get everything I intended out of each chapter. You may also want to write your answers out on a separate sheet of paper or perhaps even make a "Rejection Recovery Journal" for yourself.

For Your Personal Journey

Key Concept:

You and I were *made* by God to be loved. When we don't receive love properly, we experience the damage of rejection and develop a bad root in our lives, which feeds everything we do.

Questions:

- Can you remember your first (big) instance of experiencing real rejection? Write down your thoughts and feelings about that instance.
- Ask God to speak to you about His perspective on this instance and what He wants to say to you *today* about it.
- Write down what God says as you listen and think about the event that comes to you.

Chapter 2

EXPOSING THE REAL ENEMY

～

The primary principle behind this book is that rejection's ultimate work is guided by a spiritual force—that of the kingdom of darkness, including satan himself and then his demons. There is a person(ality) behind rejection. I realize that many people reading this book may not be comfortable with discussing demons. Some may not even believe in them. But as I will show you, demons and satan himself (or Lucifer as he was called) are real and cause real effects on humans.

Satan has endured some of the worst rejection in history. He was kicked out of the glory of heaven because he wanted to be God. When he left heaven, he was given a void and formless earth to roam as his home, but he was not yet allowed to *rule* the earth. That would be given to him later when Adam handed it to him upon his disobedience, which satan himself confirmed when he tempted Jesus in Luke 4:6.

Then, to make matters worse, God made the earth beautiful and made beautiful beings to live there that were so much like God it made satan jealous and reawakened his rejection from God.

Now, that would have been bad enough, but after God made these new creatures in His image and in His likeness, He then told them that *they* will rule the earth and have dominion over it (Genesis 1:26). Satan was probably watching all of this and didn't like the idea of this beautiful couple ruling him! After all, he had been *the* covering cherub, which is a class of beings even higher than angels, and he lived in the very presence of God.

"You were the anointed cherub who covers…"
—Ezekiel 28:14a

Since he was a created being like the animals, satan didn't yet know what Adam and Eve could or couldn't do. But he had to find out. Lucifer had not lost his *ambition*, but he had lost his *authority*. God gave all the authority on earth to Adam and Eve and satan didn't like it. Satan's ambition drove him. Remember, he had said, "I will exalt myself above the *stars* of God…I will sit on the mount of assembly" (Isaiah 14:13).

I believe that the stars of God, which are mentioned throughout scripture, are highly exalted beings that were very likely even above Lucifer and the other cherubs. Satan wanted to be above even them. This "mount of assembly" is possibly *the* mountain of God where He had His own secret council (assembly) with these stars. It is interesting to note that this mountain is mentioned in both passages regarding satan's fall—Ezekiel 28 and Isaiah 14. Satan wanted to be above these stars and put his own throne up with or in place of God's throne. Yes, he had his own throne, which is a place of rule and authority (see Isaiah 14:13). He was no small critter!

Now Satan did, I am sure, notice that Adam couldn't find a suitable helper in the animals and that God made woman to help him. One can make a healthy guess that satan would start his work on Eve since he had seen that she didn't receive all the instructions directly from God as Adam had. Satan must have assumed in his pride the woman to be weaker or lesser than man since she was created after him. But what would be his approach with her? What could he do to the new and perhaps very powerful rulers who had been given authority to rule this wonderful planet? Could he just waltz up and say, "Hi, I was the great covering cherub in heaven and, even though I got kicked out by the Guy who just made you, I am in charge"? Satan obviously decided against this sort of frontal attack.

Remember, satan was a spirit-being. He was still a cherub. But he had no physical body and he knew that in this new, physical, earth realm, one had to have a *body* to have *authority*. So when he heard and saw all that God had done with Adam and Eve, he had to find a way to stop it. After all, he wanted to be in charge of something! This pride would lead him to rejection yet again. He not only got kicked out of heaven, but he was put beneath our feet at Calvary. Rejection will keep striving to rule, but will never be given a place at the table. It's a wrong spirit.

It's important to note that most pride in humans comes from being *first* rejected and *then* the pride is used to cover and compensate for the insecurity rejection always brings. But with satan, scripture is clear when it says, "unrighteousness was found *within* you" (Ezekiel 28:15). So in satan's case, it seems that sin originated out of his creative powers. It is called "iniquity" in the NKJV Bible because it was a twisting, bending, or perversion of that which is right. Somehow he took the beauty of his being and perverted it because he had the freewill to do so.

Rejection Comes to Earth

So we see in Genesis that satan decided to physically enter an animal (the serpent in this case) and attack Eve. But he didn't try to physically kill her. No, he heard God say that Adam had authority over all the animals, so he must have assumed Adam and Eve had *some kind* of authority over him. What could he do? Aha! That's it! Do to them what God did to him—reject them! Better yet, get *God* to reject them.

Make them doubt! Make them appear to be as unloved as he felt. *Speak* to them and lie about God! Don't start an *obvious attack*, but rather lie about *God* and their *identity*. But in order to get God to reject them, he must get them to do what he did—he must get them to rebel!

> In order to get God to reject humans, he must get them to do what he did—he must get them to rebel.

I firmly believe that when satan was cast down to earth, rejection had overwhelmed him, and for good reason. He was intimate with God in a way few, if any, creatures had ever been. He was also in charge of worship in heaven (see Ezekiel 28:13). In fact, the verses in Ezekiel and Isaiah show that he actually had musical instruments within him. If you are a Christian and have been in a wonderful worship service, you know how intimate and powerful it can be. So imagine satan as he worshipped before God with all the angels and how wonderful it would have been. We also know that he sat among the angelic councils and was a special covering cherub. How exalted was he? He was so exalted that he actually thought he could ascend the very throne of God Himself! But look what scripture says about God's judgment on him:

> "I have cast you as a profane thing from the mountain of God. I have destroyed you O covering Cherub; I cast you to the ground…and you will cease to be forever."
>
> —Ezekiel 28:16–19

Satan now tries his hardest to bring his rejection and rebellion to this new, ruling humanity. He is good at it because the Bible says iniquity, or sin, was found in him. He created, if you will, sin. His sin caused him to rebel and his rebellion caused deep rejection from God, the Father, the one who loved him the most.

So he was full of rebellion and thus full of rejection and he wanted others to feel it, too. Perhaps that's where we get the saying, "Misery loves company." Satan knew there was a connection between rebellion and rejection. He probably assumed that since God was walking on the earth in close fellowship with these new creatures (see Genesis 2), it would be hard to persuade them into outright rebellion. So satan's heart began its work and, typical of his nature, he spread lies. He lied about God, wanting them to *think* that God had deceived them in some way because he knew that once someone *feels* deceived, they would *feel* rejected. He hoped that as soon as Eve felt *rejection*, she would go right into *rebellion*. Then perhaps the humans would be kicked out of this garden just like he was kicked out of heaven.

Spiritual Forces, Emotional Reality

Now you may say all this devil stuff is crazy and perhaps you just wanted a book to make you feel better and you are not interested in all this spiritual stuff. I understand, but bear with me and you will see that rejection is a spiritual force and you are a spiritual being who can react to that force.

Would you not agree that love is a spiritual force? Is it unexplainable at times? Powerful beyond human reason? A life-changing force, even? Yet did you know that the Bible is the only religious book that states, "God *is* love" (1 John 4:8)? God is a spirit-being and His opposite is the opposite of love, which is rejection. Now most people would say hate is the opposite of love, but I submit to you that what defines a word is oftentimes the effect of *doing* that word. What is the effect of love? Feeling accepted! When you are loved, do you not feel totally accepted? And when you are rejected, don't you feel unloved, even hated? If the effect of love is feeling accepted, and God is love, then the ultimate experience is to be loved by God! The opposite, then, is also true—the worst experience in life would be to feel rejected or unloved by God.

The word *satan* in Hebrew means "adversary." So he is our and God's adversary and opposite. If God is (acceptance) love, satan is (rejection) hate. Since God is the force behind all real love, I submit to you that satan and his minions are the force behind rejection.

Bad Beginnings

Rejection is the usually the first negative spirit a child encounters. It usually stays with us our whole life unless it is cast down repeatedly and fended off by speaking the Word of God to ourselves and to that spirit. The younger or the more innocent the person is, the stronger rejection is felt. In addition, when we are younger, we do not know how to separate truth from lies and intentional versus unintentional. Many of the effects of rejection from the first few years of your life may affect you today. Even babies in the womb can receive rejection. Mothers of unwanted or unplanned babies can allow a spirit of rejection to enter the life of a child when they reject the baby in their heart because they believe the baby is causing them such a huge burden in life.

In the story of Adam and Even, notice how quickly satan tried to make our first parents, who were also the first children, feel rejected by God. Remember, up to this point satan had experienced the worst rejection known to any creature in history. He wasn't about to lick his wounds alone. He wanted others to suffer with him, and they did. I believe he was hoping for the same results as his, too. He wanted them to rebel and then get God to kick them out of the garden to get them out of his way. Well, they did rebel and they did get kicked out of the garden (or their "heaven," if you will). So it seemed that all was going well for satan. But in Genesis 3:15, God prophesied to satan, and to Adam and Eve, that one of her offspring would crush satan's head.

So satan didn't get all he wanted, but he did succeed in sowing the seed of rejection into the DNA of mankind. Until the Messiah came, humans would always feel on the outside looking in, so to speak, when it came to their relationship with God. We can learn powerful spiritual and relational lessons from seeing how satan worked on Adam and Eve.

He will work the same on you—creating doubt about God's love and intentions for you and making you afraid that God will punish you for your sins.

Note that one of the strongest marks of rejection is the feeling of being on the outside, whether it's the outside of groups of family, friends, co-workers, church members, or somewhere else. This means always feeling like you are unaccepted in any group, as though there is something wrong with you—that you're different in a bad way. That's the lie of the spirit of rejection.

Doubt and Fear

The primary path for satan to attack us with rejection is when he gets us to doubt the love of those who care for us. For most of us, that is our parents, and more specifically, our father. We know instinctively that a father is to affirm, cover, and protect us. We naturally don't expect lies or deception from a parent. Eve certainly didn't expect God to be telling her lies. When she first heard another voice that contradicted what God had said, she was at least confused, and at worst, she felt very, very rejected. Remember, she was as innocent as a newborn babe in regards to rejection and sin. It was only after this smooth-talking satan told her that God had lied to her that she felt this alleged rejection.

The *very first* words satan said (never underestimate the power of words) to Eve were, "Has God said…?" (Genesis 3:1). He insinuates that their Father was not telling the truth. Do we not all feel rejected when we are lied to? Of course we do. Being lied to is another way of saying, "You have little or no value." It breeds fear, mistrust, and often anger. This is the first thing Eve heard from someone who was not either her Father or her husband.

> Satan will create doubt about God's love and intentions for you and make you afraid that God will punish you for your sins.

Secondly, satan asked, "Has God said, 'You shall *not*....'"? (Genesis 3:1). In other words, satan was saying to her that her Father was holding out on her, holding back, cheating her from something good. This is *passive rejection*. This is a very important concept to grasp if you are to understand rejection in your life! God did not attack or hit or physically hurt His first children, but once they believed the devil that He had withheld love, provision, blessings, and generally good things from them, then they *felt* that they had been rejected. The devil couldn't point to an open act of rejection from God, since that kind of accusation would have been too easy to discern as false. No, he went for a subtler approach. He suggested some act of "omission" on God's part, some indifference, which we all know can really hurt when it is discovered. The devil was trying to say, "God is not giving you all the truth about that tree."

Also notice that satan first tried to see what Eve knew about the word/command/instruction of God as it was at that time. He started off with a test, as he will with you. Satan said, "Did God *really* say...?" (NCV). Satan was emphasizing this because he is a legalist and wants to try to "catch" God and put Eve at odds with Him and His words. Eve tried to fend off this assault with the truth about God's care for them by repeating to this serpent the command of her Father. She said, "From the fruit of the trees of the garden *we may eat*; but from the fruit of the tree in the middle of the garden, God has said, 'You shall not eat from it or touch it, or you will die'" (Genesis 3:2–3).

So she did know about the truth, but she did not yet have the *conviction of the truth*. To know about a command is different than to live and obey a command. But God knew they must be tested in order for Him to have true love from His children. Untested love is no love at all; it is theory only. Love untried is empty—only an emotional thought. Once love has been challenged and upheld, then it fulfills its promise.

Because the devil saw that she knew God's word, he hit her with a full frontal assault, checking to see what strength of conviction she had.

Look at verse 4, where, in most translations, there is an exclamation point when satan responds to Eve: "You will not surely die!" (Genesis 3:4, NKJV). The Hebrew language correctly allows for this exclamation point and thus satan was *really* trying to challenge her (and God, again).

The Unholy Trinity—Lies, Rejection, and Fear

One can sense satan's boldness and Eve's fear at this point. Fear weakens us because it creates an unknown in our lives—the proverbial what-if. All the translations I have seen on Genesis 3:4 show the exclamation point in this verse, since Hebrew can show force of voice. One of satan's most common and often-effective tactics is intimidation. Intimidation is a very common tactic of those who reject us. I can just imagine, subjectively of course, satan's tone and even suspect how he would have leaned his face into hers, snarled a bit and said with some force, "You shall surely *not* die!"

This intimidation puts fear in the hearts of those listening. At this point in their interaction, Adam should have stepped in and ended the conversation, exerting his God-given authority over creation by rebuking the devil. But we know that didn't happen. Whether Eve was intimidated into sin or angry because she thought that God had lied to her, we'll never know. But experience says it was one of the two, if not both. When satan contradicted God's command with the bold statement, "You shall surely not die," Eve believed that God had lied to her and felt rejected. Fear always follows rejection: "If God lied about the tree, what else was He lying about?" Can you see how this works?

> Passive rejection can make us live a life of doubt about God's love, care, and provision.

The spirit of rejection that was deep in the heart of satan had already begun its work on Eve. Upon hearing satan say that she wouldn't die, Eve *felt* rejected by God. Wouldn't you?

She was now hearing another story from this creature and it wasn't what her Father God had said. She must have felt cheated. Eve now perceived God, not this serpent, as the liar. Now you and I know it was a lie, but again I remind you that she had never heard the voice of any other intelligent being other than her loving Father God and her husband. She was truly as innocent as a newborn babe, but God, as a wise Father, knew the test must take place. As a parent, I want to guard my children's innocence as long as I can, but I know the day will come when they must choose good over evil on their own.

A key concept here is that even passive rejection can make us live a life of doubt about God's love, care, and provision. Being lied to is a strong form of rejection. When we are lied to, we take on rejection, and then fear follows.

Feelings Lead to Action

Eve moved into rebellion after she felt rejection from God. Perhaps her thoughts went like this: "God is not fair! Why did He tell me I *would* die when I will *not* die if I eat this fruit? It looks delicious, and I bet it tastes great, too!"

Anger and resentment set in with the feeling of being set aside, unworthy of God's full disclosure. In a word, she felt *rejected*. But it didn't stop with Eve slumping into doubt and despair. It normally doesn't with us either, although that is a common reaction for some. No, this *feeling of rejection* led to the *action of rejection*, which is often disobedience or rebellion. The feeling led to the action. It almost always does. It's how we justify most sin, "I'm hurt, so I deserve a break." Of course, she was not really rejected by anyone. She *believed* she was rejected, and she believed a lie, as we all often do. That is why I tell you

> The *feeling of rejection* leads to the *action of rejection,* which is often disobedience or rebellion.

there is a spiritual source behind much of what we perceive as hurt and wounding. Jesus knew that source and called satan the father of lies (John 8:44).

Eve probably thought things such as, "Well, I'll show Him, holding out on me like that…hmmph! I'll just eat this fruit and give some to Adam, too. Then we will see what's what around here!" Sound far-fetched? I don't think so. I have had those same thoughts when I have felt rejected by a loved one, and I don't think you and I are much different than our original parents. I do know we are fighting the same enemy. The devil wants you and me to feel and actually *experience* the same rejection he did. If he can get you to act on what you feel, even if it's based on a lie, he's won! It's as simple as this: when we *think* a friend or loved one has told us a lie, we perceive the rejection and then do something to hurt them. After all, it's only fair, right? It takes great self-control and security not to retaliate. It takes the power of love.

> If the devil can get you to act on what you feel, even if it's based on a lie, he's won!

The point in this scenario is this: The attack of rejection is to get us to *doubt our caretakers' love*, be it parents, friends, or God Himself—the true caretaker.

The Separation of Rejection

Do you remember being punished by your parents as a child? Perhaps, like me, you went into your room and said in your heart, "My parents hate me. They don't love me." Or perhaps you said things like, "I hate my parents because they are punishing me." I remember pounding my pillow and saying really bad things about my parents simply because I *thought* they rejected me. We often take rejection into our heart from someone who, in reality, loves us. And even if they don't love us or didn't at the time of the hurt, we should remind ourselves that God loves us no matter what humans do. Sadly, many of us were not raised in homes that taught us the Word of God as a child, and thus, we often believe in our hearts that those we look up to have rejected us when they are disciplining us. This then leads to feelings that we are bad, unwanted, and undesirable. Next, anger and imbedded resentment set into our hearts, which leads to judgment. This is exactly what the devil wants.

When we believe someone does not care about us, then it's easy to sin against him or her. This is the division that causes such pain in our world, pitting one against the other instead of against our real adversary. Satan knows if we are united, we are powerful, especially against him. Remember the tower of Babel? It was said of their unity: "Behold they are *one* people, [of one heart and one mind], and now nothing shall be impossible for them" (Genesis 11:6). Satan knows that when we are united for God and against him, he is defeated.

As I mentioned earlier, there are basically four responses to rejection. Let me review them for you again. They are:

- Doubt and fear
- Anger or rebellion
- Withdrawal and shutdown
- Denial

Though we have primarily dealt with the first one, which is how rejection leads to doubt and fear and then to sin in our lives, we'll get to the other three. You may be saying at this point, "When I get hurt, I get depressed, but I don't get even or angry, and I don't doubt God's love." No problem, we'll cover that, but at some point we have all gotten angry and gotten even. Your "getting even" might have been to withdraw or depress yourself as a form of withholding affection from a loved one. That is still doubt, and that is still getting even; it's just turned inward, sending passive rejection back at your real or perceived rejecter.

Discern the Lie

When you feel rejected by someone, you feel hurt, angry, bitter, and cheated. Perhaps the other person was truly wrong and you feel justified in your resentment. At this point, the Spirit of God and the enemy (demon spirits) are at war in your *thought life*. Each side is going to try to get you to agree with them. One is right; one is wrong. Your agreement in the "spirit of your mind" (Ephesians 4:23) is the key to either allowing yourself to feel rejected or to forgive others and become secure in God.

The enemy will come in and lie to us about ourselves and what others think about us. The thoughts the enemy throws your way sound something like, "They don't really love you." This one always comes first and foremost. Then it's, "You're not wanted, not attractive, not loved, not accepted, not as smart as her, not as successful as him, not as desirable as that one, not as pretty as that girl, not as anointed as that minister, not as spiritual as that other Christian, will never have enough money, will never be successful," and on and on. The list is endless and brutal. Basically, rejection will raise a bar of achievement that you will never attain. It's a black hole of failure, of not measuring up in some way. Can you relate?

But doubt is the beginning of rejection. If rejection can get you to doubt the love of those around you, then where does one turn? To God of course, but we often only turn to God as a last resort. But God didn't put you here alone. He *did* intend for you to get some love from those around you in your life. It's normal to want the love of your close relationships, and it's just as normal to be hurt when you don't get it. But beware of what I call the *first doubt*. Right after the rejection comes, you will be tempted to say, "He/she doesn't love me." Just hold that thought and do what the Bible says, "Go and be reconciled to your brother" (Matthew 5:23–26).

> Doubt is the beginning of rejection. If rejection can get you to doubt the love of those around you, then where does one turn?

The second immediate companion to doubting a loved one's love for you is fear. Most people who have suffered a lot of rejection struggle with fear—fear of being alone, fear of more rejection, and fear of failure are the most common. You should note that the Bible says that one answer to fear is love since "Perfect (mature or complete) love casts out fear" (1 John 4:8, AMP).

The Doubt and Fear Progression

I stated that doubt and fear were the two first reactions to rejection. Let's watch the progression with our first parents:

- Eve doubts God's love, since she thinks God didn't tell her the whole truth about that tree.
- Eve doubts that God will take care of her needs and that His love is incomplete.
- Eve fears being on her own and thus takes things into her own hands.
- *Fear* causes her to hide from the very thing she and Adam needed—love, protection, and provision that only God could have provided.

Now let's examine what this all led to:

And the eyes of them both were opened and they knew that they were naked and they sewed fig leaves together and made themselves aprons. And they heard the Lord God walking in the garden in the cool of the day; and Adam and his wife **hid themselves** from the presence of the Lord God among the trees of the Garden. And the Lord God called unto Adam and said unto him, "Where are you?" And he said, "I heard your voice in the garden and I was **afraid**, because I was naked and hid myself. —Genesis 3:7

If you live a life filled with fear, panic, or anxiety, I can tell you the source of the problem—you need a greater revelation of the love of God in your heart. I know it sounds too simple. I had the same thought too! Let's look again at 1 John 4:18, which says it this way:

> There is no fear in love, for perfected [mature] love casts out fear; for fear has torment. He that fears is not [yet] made perfect [mature, complete] in love.

If you live a life filled with fear, panic, or anxiety, I can tell you the source of the problem—you need a greater revelation of the love of God in your heart.

The Amplified Bible says it this way:

> There is no fear in love (dread does not exist) but full-grown (complete, perfect) love turns fear out of doors and expels every trace of terror! For fear brings with it the thought of punishment, and (so) he who is afraid has not reached the full maturity of love, (is not grown into love's complete perfection).

Remember, our desire to be loved and accepted is one of, if not the strongest desire that we have. When that need is not met, it can lead to trouble. Just what kind of trouble is up to us.

So it was natural for Adam and Eve to fear because as the verse above states that fear brings with it the thought of punishment. When we feel rejected by someone, we assume that we might be punished, firstly by our parents and secondly by God. It's in our nature to assume so. And of course there is truth there, just not all the truth. God does ultimately have to punish sin and if we are one (or united) with our sin, having not been cleansed from our sin by faith in Jesus, then we do doubt God's satisfaction with us and we do have a dread of His punishment. Like Eve, we have all listened to lies and broken the commands of God. But God has a dilemma: *He does not want to punish us!* His greatest desire as a Father is to love us, but sin produces a separation. He must destroy the thing that destroys us and separates us from Him.

That is why Jesus actually became sin on the cross for us. Check out this amazing verse and the life changing truth therein:

> "He who knew no sin, became sin, on our behalf, that we might become the righteousness of God in Him [Jesus]."
> —2 Corinthians 5:21

So now with sin completely out of the way, God can love us completely. The problem is that even most Christians don't really know that sin is completely and totally out of the way, so they doubt God's perfect love for them! They still think that if they sin, God cannot completely and utterly bless them despite that sin. That may sound like heresy, but it's true. Once you are born again, all your sins—past, present, and future—are actually already taken care of. The only reason we confess our sins (see 1 John 1:9) is to restore fellowship with our Father. *We* are the ones who feel distant from *Him* when we sin. Why? Because we expect *punishment* and *judgment*! But in Romans 5:9 it says, "Much more, having been justified by His blood we shall be saved from the wrath [punishment] of God through Him [Jesus]."

> God does love you— ultimately, infinitely, wholly, and to the very end of all things, no matter what you have done.

The fear resulting from rejection will have you always looking over your shoulder or waiting for the other shoe to drop, as the old sayings go. You *expect* bad things to happen. Why? Because you are not loved (so you think) and if you are not loved, then you are not cared for; and if one is not cared for, one naturally fears. We feel naked, exposed, unsafe, and at the whim of the evil world. It's not good. But God does love you—ultimately, infinitely, wholly, and to the very end of all things, no matter what you have done. Psalm 103:10 says, "He has not dealt with us according to our sins," and all I can say is thank God! He will care for you and you need not fear.

Love Versus Fear

God's love is often not real to you and me unless we pursue its knowledge. Our heads often easily grasp the concept of God loving us, but it almost always misses our hearts. It's like knowing that God is powerful. This is easy to grasp initially in our heads; after all, just look at the universe. He must be powerful to create all this, but then we really say in the quiet desperation of our hearts, "Will His power be displayed in *my* life? Will God heal me? Will God do a miracle for me?" Rejection wants you to believe, "No!" If you remember who is ultimately behind rejection—satan, the father of lies—then you'll begin to see that he wants you to believe the lie that you are not worthy of God's power, love, and protection.

> The rules of God never produce love and faith, but the love of God always produces faith in our hearts.

The enemy of your soul doesn't mind if you fear or reverence God. He doesn't even mind if you worship God at church and praise Him. But satan really doesn't want you to believe that God loves you. If you believe God loves you, then you will begin to receive God's miracles of healing, provision, and joy and *that* will be a physical demonstration to the world that God is real and that God loves them, too. Satan definitely doesn't want that. This is why people thronged to be around Jesus—they knew He loved them. He proved it by healing their bodies, encouraging them that God cared for them. The Pharisees of the day, the Jewish leaders, only reminded people that they were not obeying all the rules of Jewish law. But this produced fear, not faith. The rules of God never produce love and faith, but the love of God always produces faith in our hearts.

In Wayne Jacobson's excellent book *He Loves Me*, he writes the following:

> Fear cannot lead us to a lifelong transformation, but only a momentary reformation of behavior. Instead of inviting us to enter into a relationship with a living God, it pushes us away with feelings of inadequacy and repetitious failure.[4]

He later states that the fear of the Lord is the beginning of wisdom, as Proverbs 1 says, but it's only the *beginning*—love is the fulfillment (completion) of wisdom.[5] I would say that love inspires me to draw near to Him who is Wisdom. Love always attracts and fear always separates.

In Genesis, we see God walking in the garden with Adam and Eve and *calling out to them*, wanting the fellowship, relationship, and intimacy they had so enjoyed. Imagine the Father's heart when He heard His children saying that they were afraid of Him. As a father, it would pain me beyond belief to see my children withdraw in fear from me, in mistrust and anxiety, doubting my love. To have my children doubt my care for them would be a great pain indeed. Yet that is exactly what happened. Why? They felt rejected, lied to, and cheated. Of course they felt that way, because they believed a lie! But it didn't change their emotions or, sadly, their actions!

Fear—Faith Upside Down

Fear will be the natural result of rejection because you and I expect to no longer be loved. My friend, whether you know it or not, if you expect your life to be one without love, you will be fearful and very anxious. So the second emotion we see in our first parents was fear. Doubt almost always leads to some kind of fear.

Did you know that fear is the same thing as faith, only backwards, upside down, and twisted? Fear is the same *force* as faith, only it's faith in evil or bad things, whereas true faith is the expectation of good things. Faith *expects* something, and if it doesn't expect, then it's just hope and not faith. The Bible's definition is this:

> Faith is the substance of things hoped for, the evidence of things not seen. —Hebrews 11:1

Rejection leads to fear of more rejection. The expectation of rejection is just like the force of faith, but perverted. Faith expects acceptance, love, and friendship with God and man. The Bible says in that same chapter of Hebrews that, "Without faith, it's impossible to please God, for those who believe in Him know that He is a *rewarder* of those who diligently seek Him (Hebrews 11:6). Yes, God rewards, here and now! He blesses, here and now!

But a root of rejection will expect or dread bad things—broken relationships, failure at work, and generally a life of gloom. You may even fear punishment here and now from God! I know at one point I did. Even though I knew I was His child, I had a warped faith—it's called fear—and it caused me to expect God to whack me whenever I sinned. I knew better in my head, but that didn't change the *emotion* of my heart or spirit. It took some healing to "reverse the curse," as they say.

Adam and Eve hid from God. Do we not hide from others when we feel rejected? Of course we do. We withdraw and change our persona to avoid more rejection. We put on an air of pretense, appearing to be someone we are not, all to be accepted because we see ourselves as rejected. Our self-image, like that of our first parents, has changed when we believe that we are damaged goods.

That is natural in our fallen state, but God can correct this behavior by filling us with His love. For just as God immediately made provision for His two children by providing skins to cover their newfound nakedness, He also promised a Savior to crush satan, which was the real source of their pain. Their Father provided for them both short and long-term, as we see in Genesis. It's important to note that just as He then protected them from living eternally in that fallen state, so too will God provide love to you. He will fulfill His promise for a Savior and He will protect you by giving you eternal life in heaven. I call it the *three P's of the Garden*—Provision, Protection, and Promise.

Fear and Self-Rejection

Also note that the rejection that our first parents perceived *caused them to dislike themselves.* They didn't like the way they looked and covered themselves. Rejection tells us we are unlovable, unacceptable, and that we will live that way forever. It creates hopelessness for a loving future if we don't know the love and provision of God, for God will always provide love for us if we are willing to reach out to Him.

Fear of being alone will also be a force that comes with rejection. We will experience either a general paranoia of being alone or the fear of being single and without a spouse or close friends. Those who suffer panic attacks are almost always people rooted in rejection and trauma who have yet to get a spiritual revelation of the love of our Father God.

I remember at one point in my life when I couldn't get a date no matter how hard I tried, so much so that I began to live in this funk of self-pity and the fear of being single my whole life, living a life of loneliness. Perhaps you are there, too. You might even be married, yet feel alone in that marriage. As you let God's love permeate your life and break the roots of rejection, you will find that things can wonderfully change. I am happy to say that I am happily married! The lie of being alone forever was just that—a lie!

Think about your fears and ask yourself if and how they relate to the rejection in your life. Then begin to ask God to show you areas of rejection you are not aware of. It will most often start with parents and close family members and branch out from there.

If you suffer from panic and anxiety, did you know and experience a close, loving father, one who provided for you, protected you, and fulfilled his promises to you? Probably not. Start to meditate on this thought: God, the ultimate loving Father, has *not* rejected you. I know He may seem distant, mystical, unreachable, and too aloof now, but He can become very, very real in your life.

> You and I can now walk free from rejection and the fear it leads to because of the unconditional acceptance we have from God.

Whenever I doubt God's love, I look to the cross on which Jesus died. I remind myself of 1 John 4:18 that says, "Perfect love casts out fear." I also look to the next verse, which states something that is key, "We love because *He first* loved us." God reached out to humanity *first* by becoming a man and loving us enough to take our sins into His own spirit and body so that we could once again "walk in the cool of the day" in the Garden of Heaven forever. Not bad, huh?

Another verse says, "While we were yet sinners, Christ died for us," and again, "We have peace with God, through our Lord Jesus Christ," and, "Having been justified by His blood we shall be free from wrath through Him" (Romans 5:1, 8–9).

Adam and Eve cowered in fear after their sin, which resulted from *feeling* rejected by God. You and I can now walk free from rejection and the fear it leads to because of the unconditional acceptance we have from God. But think about how often you reject God's commandments because you already are feeling rejected by life. We get these thoughts that say, *Well I'm just an old crusty sinner anyway. I've blown it so bad, I might as well just keep going and sin some more. After all, God (and everyone else) has rejected me, so why not live like the devil?* Or we think, *I might as well wallow in the mud of life, since I am just a pig.* Can you relate? I know I have had those thoughts—many times. But they are a lie. Remember, satan has not stopped lying to humanity; we have all believed lies about ourselves. God has never rejected you and many people whom you think have rejected you actually may still offer love to you if the relationship will be tended to and healed. The devil is the one who wants you to give up on love, which is the ultimate rejection, *to believe there is nothing good or lovely in this life.*

Tina Turner got it wrong in her song, "What's Love Got to Do With It?" Love has got everything to do with the fact that God is love, and God has everything to do with us. Tina Turner suffered a lot of abuse and betrayal in her life and it's no wonder she could sing that song. But she was wrong when she crooned, "It's just a second-rate emotion." No, love is not second rate and it's not just an emotion. It's the very nature of God and it's what makes life worth living. Love causes us to do good in life and put off evil!

In the movie *The Lord of the Rings* when Frodo asks Sam at the very end how they could possibly go on, Sam said, and I paraphrase, "Because I have to believe there is some good in the world, that good will prevail over this darkness and evil, and that life is worth fighting for." Rejection and fear say the opposite, but don't believe them. Love is worth the effort and God does love you despite your feelings today!

FOR YOUR PERSONAL JOURNEY

Key Concept:

When we *perceive* rejection, we feel cheated, angry, and hurt and often do what Eve did—rebel against God and man.

Question:

- What lies or misconceptions about God and His care for you have entered your life as a result of perceiving or experiencing rejection?

CHAPTER 3

REJECTION AND SPIRITUAL WARFARE

Often people who are not familiar with what Christianity calls *deliverance* will ask, "Can rejection really be a spirit," or, "Aren't these feelings just bad memories?" (Deliverance can also be known as *exorcism*, or the *expelling of demons* from people's lives.) Certainly not all bad memories or hurtful feelings are demons or even demonic in nature. As mentioned in my booklet *Demons, Angels, and Deliverance*, the telltale sign of a spirit's influence are *out-of-control* feelings, thoughts, fears, and anxieties or any other *out-of-control* behavior.

The fear of rejection can control your life, or past rejections can control your life today by how they have affected your personality or emotions (soul). So yes, you can be "out of control" because of a spirit of rejection, meaning that your reactions are not what you *know* to be godly because of a spirit that lingers on to exercise its power over you. Please keep an open mind as we explore the realty of a *spirit* of rejection and spiritual warfare against humans.

The Spirit World is a Reality!

The main thing to be clear on is this: there is a spirit world and it's just as real as the physical world. Most people instinctively know this, but choose to live their life with very little interaction with this world... until they *have* to. Right off in Genesis we see the Spirit of God hovering over the waters. In John 4:24, Jesus declares to us that God is Spirit. All throughout scripture, we see that man is also a spirit, as noted in Ecclesiastes 12:7 where it says the "departed spirits [of man] will return to God." We will see more on this later, but know that as spirits, *we are always in the spirit world* whether we like it or not. As a human, you are spirit, soul, and body as 1 Thessalonians 5:23 says. As such, you are a creature that exists 100 percent in the spirit world *and* 100 percent in the natural world *at the same time.* So when

> You are a creature that exists 100 percent in the spirit world *and* 100 percent in the natural world *at the same time.*

it comes to warfare, we also have both natural (physical) wars and spiritual wars. Satan is the "god of this world" as 2 Corinthians 4:4 states, and his number one tool against you is rejection!

The Bible calls satan the "prince of the power of the air," but I like to call him the prince of rejection since it was satan who experienced total rejection when he was kicked out of heaven. He is still licking his wounds and wants you to feel the same rejection he still feels. He knows how effective it was against Eve, as we discussed earlier, so he will continue to work his evil on us today. What is his end game? It is to make you think God has rejected or will reject you! He truly knows how powerful rejection can be because he used to live in the glory of God's love and knows how horrible it feels to now be without that love. Let's look at the devil's history to better understand how he works in both the spiritual and natural realm today. It's always good to know as much about your opponent as possible.

Thus says the Lord God: "You were the seal of **perfection, full** of wisdom and **perfect** in beauty. *You were in Eden, the garden of God*; every precious stone was your covering: The sardius, topaz, and diamond, beryl, onyx, and jasper, sapphire, turquoise, and emerald with gold. The workmanship of your timbrels and [musical] pipes was prepared for you on the day **you were created**. You were *the* anointed cherub who covers; I established you; *you were on the holy mountain of God*; you walked back and forth in the midst of fiery stones. You **were perfect** in your ways from the day you were created, till iniquity was found **in you**. By the abundance of your trading you became filled with violence within, and you sinned; *therefore I cast you as a profane thing out of the mountain of God*; and I destroyed you, O covering cherub, from the midst of the fiery stones. Your heart was lifted up because of your beauty; you corrupted your wisdom for the sake of your splendor; *I cast you to the ground*." —Ezekiel 28:12–17

I have emphasized the words I believe point to the fact that the person being spoken of here cannot be merely human. Note that he was in Eden, the garden of God, and on the holy mountain of God, and that he was established by God, and was called perfect. No human was in Eden *and* on the mountain of God. This is clearly satan himself and he was *the* anointed cherub, not *an* anointed cherub. He was The Dude in Heaven other than God himself! We are not dealing with some little puffball here!

Who Is This "Man"?

Now consider the following corroborating verses in Isaiah:

How you are fallen from heaven, O Lucifer, son of the morning! How you are **cut down to the ground**, you who weakened the nations! For you have said in your heart: "I will ascend into heaven, I will exalt my throne above the stars of God [stars are the other angels, see Job 38:7]; I will also sit on the mount of the congregation on the farthest sides of the north; I will ascend above the heights of the clouds, I will be like the Most High." **Yet you shall be brought down to Sheol, to the lowest depths of the Pit.** —Isaiah 14:12–15

So you see both sets of verses speak about one who was highly exalted, honored, beautiful, and powerful, yet was cast down to earth and the pit (his main and eternal home). Lucifer, or satan, endured great rejection for his sin (of pride) and is now the leader of evil spirits in this world. Lucifer, which means light-bearer, was cut down and thrust into the pit, and not just any pit, but *the pit of hell*, which the Bible says was "prepared for the devil and his angels" (Matthew 25:41). Now *that* is rejection!

Satan was once Lucifer, a chosen cherub of God. Cherubs were one of the highest order of beings, and those who enjoyed very close fellowship, even possibly friendship, with God. He was involved in worship (as noted by his timbrels of music in Ezekiel) and thus great intimacy with God. He may have been the most favored of created beings. And yet he endured the worst rejection—being cast out "as a profane thing" as Ezekiel says. It must have hurt pretty badly. So my point is this: *Rejection is satan's specialty!* He's experienced it more than any other emotion and traffics in it well. It is, in my mind, his greatest and most subtle weapon and one that we often miss as being demonic, or even spiritual.

> ~
> **Rejection is satan's specialty! It is his greatest and most subtle weapon and one that we often miss as being demonic, or even spiritual.**

Sadly, most Americans associate demonic activity with Africa or witches in huts with voodoo dolls or séances or other such things. But demons are rarely that obvious and, yes, they torment people around the world, especially Christians. They simply want to enslave and control humans for two reasons. First, they formerly had bodies and desperately want back in them to touch and experience this world again. Second, they hate God and the crowning glory of His creation and the thing that is most like Him, which is—you!

They really don't worry much about the non-Christian because that person is already in their camp, so to speak. But if the Christian ever learns their authority over them, he or she can do much damage to the demonic kingdom. Remember that Jesus predicted their demise in Mark 16 when He said that Christians shall "cast out demons," and of course they have been doing just that for over two thousand years. So of course they want Christians to either disregard them or misunderstand them so as to have no effect against them!

Get to Know Your Demon?

My book called *Demons, Angels and Deliverance* shows that spirits take on the name of the sin or *behavior* they induce people into. For example, a spirit who induces us to fear is a "spirit of fear." But not all spirits represent our sin. Sometimes we are a victim of other people's actions and the devil comes in to "plunder our house" (see Matthew 12:41–45). Many children who are sexually abused not only end up with spirits of rejection and shame, but also with a spirit of lust controlling them since that is the spirit that most often controlled the abuser. Once sexual feelings are aroused and a child experiences that, no matter how it comes, the spirit can often addict them again to it like a drug. Not that the abused child sinned and gave the devil a legal right to torment him, but the demon will take advantage of us as long as he can. Demons are, in a word, trespassers.

Just as some people are given illicit drugs unknowingly at parties and then get addicted to the high they experienced, even though they didn't ask for it, sexual abuse can often be the same. Sadly, sexual, physical, and verbal abuse will open the door to many different spirits, such as self-hatred, shame, fear, anger, and rage.

Demons are intelligent, scheming, and organized in their evil. If they can get you to live rejected and insecure and to always expect that sort of abuse, then they have achieved their goal, which is to keep you from the love of other people and ultimately from God. After all, if everyone else in life has rejected you, why wouldn't God since He is so perfect and powerful? Or so the reasoning goes. Isn't that the feeling you have had at some point in your life? "Why would *God* accept me?" You *expect* rejection from everyone else, why not God? So the spirit has trained you as it whispers lies to you and it just happened to use the humans who hurt you as its tools.

The enemy knows that God is your ultimate source of love and acceptance, so he trains you to think church, religion, Christianity, Christians, and God will all reject you, find fault with you, and judge you. That is why the number one thing non-Christians think about Christians is that they are judgmental and condemning. The first thing I hear from non-Christians when I am sharing the gospel with them is, "You're judging me." Nothing is further from the truth. It is love that causes us to share the gospel, not judgment. Yet satan and his minions have trained the world that God and His people will reject them! It's the easiest thing to convince them of *because* most humans have endured so much rejection in their life by the time the start to think about God that they expect God to reject them, too.

> Most humans have endured so much rejection in their life by the time the start to think about God that they expect God to reject them, too.

Few of us grew up expecting God to unconditionally love us. Yet the Bible says He does!

In order to understand if there actually can be a spirit of rejection, we must understand demons in general. There is no better example than the Bible. Let's see how Jesus explained the working of demons in the gospels. You might be in the same place as the Pharisees when Jesus began casting out demons. They did not at all understand how demons worked and so the only thing they could figure was that he was doing the exorcisms by the power of the devil. It never dawned on them that their God, Yahweh, had already promised that His children would be delivered from forces too powerful for them. But He did.

Look at this Old Testament example of deliverance promised in Isaiah 49:24–26:

> "Can the prey [victim] be taken from the mighty man, or the captive of a tyrant be rescued?" Surely, thus says the Lord, "Even the captives of the mighty man will be taken away, and the prey of the tyrant will be rescued, **for I will contend with the one who contends with you, and your sons**…all flesh will know that I, the Lord, am your **Redeemer**, the Mighty One of Israel."

Later in Isaiah, he previews the Messiah's mission to mankind to further help those bound with demonic influence:

> The Spirit of the Lord is upon Me, because the Lord has anointed me to preach good news to the meek, the has sent Me to bind up [heal] the broken hearted, **to proclaim liberty to the captives and the opening of the prison doors to them that are bound**." —Isaiah 61:1–2

When Jesus then started His ministry, the first thing He read was this verse (see Luke 4:17–19). After He read this verse in the synagogue, He said, "This day, this scripture is fulfilled in your sight." Jesus was saying, "I am the Promised One. Those verses in Isaiah are going to start coming to pass and I'm the one who'll do all that you read." Sure enough, Jesus began casting demons out of bound people and spent his ministry doing exactly what the prophecies said. Not only that, He said His followers would do the same.

> "These signs will follow those who have believed, in My name they will…cast out demons." —Mark 16:17

Millions of people today are "bound" or "captive" to the fear of rejection and/or the effects of past rejections in their life. The rejections or demons of rejection have trained them by lying to them for years. The incredible news is that God has overpowered satan and his demons and can now heal you and set you free!

Strong Men

When Jesus spoke of the "strong man," he was referring to the "tyrant" spoken of in Isaiah 49. We know that what was a natural or physical entity in the Old Testament foreshadowed spiritual entities in the New Testament. If you have endured severe rejection and then have subsequently continued to be rejected your whole life, or at least felt that way, you have been living under a "tyrant," or "strong man" as Jesus called him, who rules over you. The strong man is simply the influence of the strongest demon in your life.

This is why rejected people keep getting more rejection and abused people keep getting abused. They don't want more of the pain, but the demonic strong man has found a home in their house and is running the show. They are out of control. Those trained by rejection act in a way that gets more rejection because that is what they know, and believe it or not, human nature prefers a known pain over a change to something unknown.

Be honest, in your own life. Have you kept yourself on the rejection treadmill even though it hurt because you were afraid of the uncertainty of a new and different life?

In Matthew 12 and Mark 3, the Pharisees wrongly accused Jesus of using satanic powers for His deliverance ministry. Jesus explained that if this were true then satan was divided against himself and his kingdom would end. But Mark 3:27 is the important part because Jesus was trying to show them that He is the deliverer that God prom-

> *Have you kept yourself on the rejection tread-mill even though it hurt because you were afraid of the uncertainty of a new and different life?*

ised through Isaiah, and though people had demonic tyrants in their life, He could redeem (buy back) those under the tyrant's power. Remember, Isaiah 25:49 ends by saying, "I am the Mighty One of Israel," and this is not a demon talking! Jesus is teaching several things here. Let's look:

> "But no one enter the strong man's house and plunder his property unless he first binds the **strong man** and then he will plunder his house." —Mark 3:27

Matthew records it thus:

> "But if I cast out demons by **Spirit of God** then the kingdom of God has come upon you, or how can anyone enter the **strongman's house** and carry off his property, unless he first **binds** [forbids] the strong man, then he will plunder his house." —Matthew 12:28

Look at Isaiah 49:24–26 one more time:

> "Can the prey [victim] be taken from the mighty man, or the captive of a tyrant be rescued?" Surely, thus says the Lord, "Even the captives of the mighty man will be taken away, and

the prey of the tyrant will be rescued, **for I will contend with the one who contends with you, and your sons**…all flesh will know that I, the Lord, am your **Redeemer**, the Mighty One of Israel."

These verses should prompt these questions in your mind:

- What/who is a strong man?
- What is his property?
- How do you bind the strong man?
- What is his house?

Before we answer those questions, let's look at what else Jesus told us about the working of spirits:

> "Now when the unclean spirit goes out of a man, it passes through waterless places seeking rest and does not find it, then it says, 'I will return to my house from which I came'; and when it comes, it finds it unoccupied, swept clean and empty." —Matthew 12:43–44

So here are the answers to those four questions: First, what is a strong man? Simply put, it is a demon. Again, if this is new to you, you might reject that idea and believe your pain and actions are all based on memories, hurts, and such. I submit to you that both spirits and hurtful memories affect you today, but the *predominant* influence is a spirit of rejection moving you and controlling you so that you can't get free from the pattern, pain, and persistence of past and current rejections.

More than that, the strong man is the ruling demon of the group that is in your life. And you probably say, "GROUP!? You mean I can have more than one bothering me?" Oh, yes, I guarantee it! I have never met a human who hasn't had more than one spirit working on them. Jesus confirms the working of groups and even hierarchy in the satanic kingdom.

This is what Jesus said immediately following the verses quoted above:

> "Then it goes and takes along with it **seven other spirits, more wicked than itself**, and they go in and live there."
> —Matthew 12:45

So we see there is order or rank by the statement, "more wicked than itself,." So the more wicked ones are bigger, higher in rank, and more evil. The one who was cast out saw that the house has been "worked on," so it perhaps said something like this: "I need some help; this person has been praying, reading his Bible, going to counseling, and he is trying to set things right. I've got a battle going on, so I better get some help!" Then it gets some fellows to make sure you don't cast them out again. Of course the silly demons should learn that Jesus is always more powerful then they are *if the person wants to be free* (see Matthew 12:44)!

The Names of Demons

I want to show you in greater detail how demons are named so you can know there is a spirit of rejection. Notice that in Luke 11:14 it says the following:

> And He was casting out a spirit and *it was mute*; when the demon had gone out the mute man spoke; and the crowds were amazed.

Inspired by the Holy Spirit, Luke recorded in the scriptures that the demon here was a mute spirit. Was that because the *demon* couldn't speak? The answer is no, for we know they can if allowed (see Luke 8:28). Rather, it caused muteness. Yes, demons can totally affect your physical body. So a rejection spirit can cause rejection or cause a state of mind that believes that one is or always will be rejected. Just as a demon can cripple a physical body, so a spirit can cripple or corrupt your mind and emotions.

When the man who could not speak began speaking after Jesus cast out the demon, everyone knew that it was a mute spirit, or a spirit that *caused* muteness, that afflicted him. It is the same with rejection or any other torment. Demons take on the name of the affliction or sin that they incite.

Now we can't blame a demon for our sin because, as I said, they most times come in when we give them a legal right to do so and what gives them legal rights is our sin. But we can know what spirit is active in our life by the affliction or sin we are enslaved to. Those who are constantly struggling with anger, lust, jealousy, and such have either opened that door themselves *or* it can be opened by those who sin against them. We are either victims or villains, and usually both!

That is why Jesus placed so very much emphasis on forgiveness because it breaks the power of the sins against us. When you don't forgive, God can't move in your life. But when you forgive those who hurt and rejected you, God is now free to deal with both them and you. Unforgiveness of your perpetrator places a wall between them and God, and between you and God, and binds His hands from working in either their life or yours.

How Rejection Enters

There are times when someone is rejected by a loved one. At that time they will *believe* the harsh words or actions that come against them, especially if they are young. Of course demons are ready and willing to reinforce the words of rejection because they see the wounds that come our way. So they whisper all kinds of lies into our hearts. Here is a sample cycle:

- Abuse, trauma, and rejecting events happen

- Lies are spoken from fellow humans often inspired by demons
- Lies are believed
- The demons repeat the lies to us and we sadly think they are our thoughts instead of a demon's voice
- Demonic attachment and then oppression occurs (notice I didn't say possession)

Christians can't be possessed, but they can be very, very oppressed. I have seen Christians very addicted, enslaved, and tormented by ungodly addictions, sins, and thought patterns that can only be described as demonic. Many times, great Christian leaders fall and people are shocked. I am not. I know how badly leaders are attacked and how badly they can be oppressed. They are targets of the enemy day and night. *Many, many Christians get into leadership not knowing that they did so to get affirmation to heal an unknown root of rejection.* Read that again because it's a sad but powerful truth. If you know a leader who has experienced severe rejection, give him or her this book!

> Many, many Christians get into leadership not knowing that they did so to get affirmation to heal an unknown root of rejection.

Remember, because we are all part villain and part victim, *we don't sin in the area of rejection. But when we are rejected, we often turn to sin to make us feel better.* We often try in turn to reject those who hurt us, either to avoid more hurt or to make us feel in control. Rejection makes you feel out of control. After all, you didn't invite that hurt, did you? But wham, there it came—the words, the indifference, the neglect or the abuse. You didn't invite it, yet you got it. So you and I will feel out of control. Thus to feel in control or to balance our emotional equilibrium, we all like to get even. One of the most common reactions to rejection is a *vow* or *judgment* against the one who hurt us. We say things in our heart against those wounding us and really curse them and ourselves in the process. Jesus said it this way,

> "For with what judgment you judge, you will be judged; and with the measure you use, it will be measured back to you."
> —Matthew 7:2, NKJV

Trespassers

So why would a *spirit* of rejection come in? Because demons and the devil are not kind creatures; they are trespassers. They will take advantage of us when we are hurt or sinned against…if we let them. If you have been rejected, but unable to identify the rejection and forgive those who hurt you, it's possible that a spirit of rejection could hide its workings in your life and hold you in bondage, even "illegally." I say illegally because Christians have been forgiven, loved, and blessed by God and have authority over all demonic attacks. But it's the warfare you don't know about that will hurt you!

We are in spiritual warfare against demon spirits in varying ranks and orders, and unless you understand that, you will always try to fix a *spiritual* problem through *human* means. You will always look to mankind as the problem and/or the answer, instead of understanding that the real problem always lies with the spiritual. Mankind is the *instrument* of rejection, but not the *source* of it. And man can offer some help, but only the *love of God* destroys rejection in your life.

> Mankind is the *instrument* of rejection, but not the *source* of it. Man can offer some help, but only the *love of God* destroys rejection in your life.

Note the following verses:

> For though we walk in the flesh [natural or earthly senses and human condition], **we do not war according to the**

flesh. For the weapons of our warfare are **not earthly** but mighty in God for pulling down strongholds, casting down arguments and every imagination that exalts itself against the knowledge of God, bringing every thought into captivity to the obedience of Christ. —2 Corinthians 10:3-5

Put on the armor of God so that you may be able to stand firm against the tactics of the devil. For **our struggle is not with flesh and blood but** with the principalities, with the powers, with the world rulers of this present darkness, **with the evil spirits in the heavens**. —Ephesians 6:12

That you should put away the old self of your former way of life, corrupted through deceitful desires, and **be renewed in the *spirit* of your mind**. —Ephesians 4:22

We should notice two things here. First, we are at war and that war is based on what we believe about reality. Second, we are not at war with humans, but with demonic forces. They are the liars whispering those destructive thoughts in our heart day after day. Until you come to grips with this spiritual reality, you will *never* have total victory in your life and you will *never* have the peace Jesus bought for you.

You have been rejected by humans, but they are not the evil source behind that rejection. *Long* after that rejection event is over, the demons still will torment you about the rejection. Remember that your rejecter was probably driven by demons and tormented themselves. Even after the people who first and most hurt you are dead, the enemy of our souls will try to cause you to live rejected. Only Jesus has the power to heal our memories and minds from rejection. Remember, He specifically said, "I came to heal the broken hearted" (Isaiah 61:1; Luke 4:18). Isn't that the ultimate work of rejection? To make you feel you have a broken, fractured, misunderstood heart?

Prayer and Warfare

Most every person you will meet will admit that they have prayed for God to help them at one point in their lives. If you have been rejected much in life, you may have prayed more than the average person. There is one other example of spiritual warfare I would like you to look at in regards to demons and humans and how this all plays out in our lives.

Have you ever felt like God didn't answer your prayers? I have, a lot. But at least I know why, for most of them anyway. There are great beings out there (demons) stopping those who are the agents of answering our prayers (angels). We are called upon to pray for ourselves and others and expect, in faith, the Lord to answer our prayers. But you may be reading this book because you have not had your prayers answered, at least as far as you can tell. You are still struggling with pain, hurt, wounds, and bad feelings and you want help. You want more *victory*! So do I!

Many people turn to deliverance as a last resort. It usually comes after personal prayer, counseling, Bible study, and some type of drugs or medicines, none of which am I in any way against. But we should be doing deliverance prayer first and then asking God to show us why things are not changing.

If He directs us to medicine or counsel, that is fine. But most people won't even discuss deliverance when it comes to rejection. Yet, as I have pointed out, rejection is the number one thing satan endured and it's the number one thing he wants you to feel, especially from God! It's his *first* line of attack. It starts in the womb and goes from there with parents, then siblings, then schoolmates, then girlfriends or boyfriends, then spouses, then your own kids, and ultimately your church friends who are supposed to be your second family. Church is supposed to be safe, yet much rejection is endured in the church!

Look at Daniel 10 to see the kind of opposition we can face when we pray. The backdrop is this: Daniel had been fasting and praying for three weeks and saw a great vision but had no understanding. The angel that was originally sent to answer his prayers was *delayed* for three weeks by the "prince of Persia."

> Then he said to me, "Do not fear, Daniel, for from the first day that you set your heart to understand, and to humble yourself before your God, your words were heard; and I have come because of your words. But the prince of the kingdom of Persia withstood me twenty-one days; and behold, Michael, one of the chief princes, came to help me, for I had been left alone there." —Daniel 10:12–13

This prince of Persia was not a physical human prince, but a spiritual one. Note that Paul in his epistles mentions "principalities" several times when listing demonic hierarchy. When we pray, the enemy tries to stop or hinder our prayers and angels are the agents used to answer our prayers. Note that the angel said to Daniel, "I have come because of your words." Our words and prayers create spiritual warfare and when we began to pray for healing from rejection, shame, fear, and anxiety, we enter the battle, so to speak. But the great and awesome news is this: Jesus won the war!

> Our words and prayers create spiritual warfare. When we began to pray, we enter the battle. But the great and awesome news is this: Jesus won the war!

> He raised Him from the dead and seated Him at His right hand in the heavenly places, far above all principality and power and might and dominion, and every name that is named, not only in this age but also in that which is to come. And He put all things under His feet, and gave Him to be head over all things. —Ephesians 1:20–22

When you see the words *dominion*, *principality*, *might*, *powers*, or *authorities* in the letters of Paul, he is referring to demonic spirits. But God declares here that we are above them if we are in Jesus.

Our Victory

Colossians 2:15 states, "Having disarmed principalities and powers, He made a public spectacle of them, triumphing over them in [the cross]." Jesus utterly defeated all the powers of darkness. So no matter what spirit, or human for that matter, has or will come against you in life, Jesus has the answer and Jesus is the answer. Jesus defeated ALL evil, period!

You may be frustrated, tired, hopeless, angry, and depressed at the lack of success in dealing with rejection or whatever else is ailing you in your emotions. In fact, you may not even be sure that rejection is the root of your issues. That is okay. I have been doing this long enough to tell you one thing for sure—*God* absolutely knows about your pain and *cares* about your pain. Let me give you some examples of a God who knows us all.

Recently on a ministry trip I was eating at a café when the Lord told me the waitress had just had her heart broken by a man in her life. When I went up to her and asked her if that were true, she tearfully said yes. She said she wanted to go out drinking with her friends to numb the pain. But Jesus had a better plan. He wanted to show her a better way as He does for you! God knew all about her pain, her heartache, and simply used me to tell her that He was aware of it and that she needed to turn to Him for help. We prayed for her and got her hooked up with a local church. I have had that happen more times than I can count. I know that if God knows about that waitress, He knows about you and your pain.

At another restaurant, as I spoke to the waitress, she began to tell me how her life was full of guilt and shame and she didn't know why. Suddenly the Lord spoke to me and told me it was her mother. I then told her, "I know the why you struggle with guilt and shame."

Shocked, she said, "You do?"

I said, "Yes, it's your mother."

Her eyes opened wide and she said, "Oh my [blankety blank], you're right; how did you know that?"

I said, "God told me, and He showed me that your mother constantly demeaned you with her words. You could never live up to her standards and she was constantly critical of you." She said that was exactly right and then she prayed with us, with tears in her eyes, to accept the Lord into her heart.

God knows and cares about all your pain. Open your mind and heart and see if the following pages will give you some clues as to how rejection works in our lives and how you can be free from its effects.

Perhaps all this demon talk is scary to you, or maybe it's just uncomfortable. I understand. I grew up Catholic and the only time we talked about demons was when the infamous priest and demon in the movie *The Exorcist* came up in our occasional "spiritual" conversations. When you see what the Bible says about your authority over demons (as a Christian), this whole topic will pose no fear to you but rather give you great insight into the workings of our world.

Demons Are Not the Point

My point is not to focus on demons, but to make sure we understand our opponent. Our warfare is not against flesh and blood. My parent's rejection of me had an evil force behind it and though they are accountable for giving in to it, I have the ability to love them by recognizing that it is the demons themselves that inspired the thoughts, words, and deeds that hurt me. Also, once you recognize a spirit of rejection in your life, it will always have the same patterns and so you will be able to defend yourself in the future and help others who have come under its influence.

When I was single, I used to suffer from self-pity to a point of almost a total state of despondency, lethargy, and depression in regards to ever getting married or even getting a date! Then one day it dawned on me that I was dealing with a *spirit* of self-pity. Of course I loathed the idea that I was communing with a demon, but I knew it was true. I saw the pit it was dragging me into—the out-of-control self-pity—and I immediately began to rebuke it and back out of that pit. In a short while I was free from it and was then very sensitive to when those thoughts and emotions were coming on me. It was like a drug, and when it tried to get near me, I rebuked it and eventually that thing knew the gig was up! Once a demon knows that you know what is really going on, it's on its way out!

But as long as it can get you to look to anything but spiritual deliverance, it will stay and hide. For a season drugs may mask it, sex may mask it, money may mask it, but only finding, binding, and casting out the strongman and its cohorts will set you free. Of course the way to stay free is to focus on the person of Jesus of Nazareth and not at the demon!

So open your heart, study the life and ministry of Jesus, and ask God to show you about some of the spiritual realities in the Bible. If you do, you will begin to learn how the world works when it comes to spirit versus human struggles.

For the sake of clarity, let me say that I do *not* believe every problem or issue in our lives is demonic. For example, if I run around in my underwear in a cold rainstorm and get sick, I am not going to blame the devil, though I will still pray to God for healing due to His great love and mercy to help me even when I am silly. But when it comes to finding solutions for our lives, as Westerners we err far more on the side of dismissing the supernatural than we do engaging the supernatural.

Is This *Really* a Demon?

At this point many people ask, "How can I *identify* whether or not my feelings are from a *spirit* of rejection?" Here some questions to ask yourself to identify if a spirit of rejection is harassing you:

- Do you continually believe people don't like you?
- Do you have continual thoughts of failure or fear of failure that prevent you from trying?
- Is the glass half empty rather than half full?
- Are you anti-social for fear of rejection?
- Do have a hard time accepting God's love for you or other friends/family member's love?
- Is it hard to receive compliments or gifts?
- Do you always think people are staying away from you, but you can't pinpoint why?
- Do you often feel condemnation even when, in examining your heart, you can't find unconfessed sin?
- Do you often take comments personally that others do not?
- Do you often feel anger as a result of not feeling accepted by those whom you want to accept/acknowledge you?
- Do you often withdraw from those whom you actually want acceptance from because they are not receiving you as you wish?
- Does recalling your relationship with your parents, especially your father, bring back hurtful memories?
- Is there ongoing pain in memories of them saying hurtful things to you?
- Can a negative word from them still wound you?
- Are you constantly failing or falling short in your mind?

- Do you often feel needy or feel others withdraw from you because you want too much?
- Do you always feel on the outside looking in? When family, friends, or coworkers gather, do you very often feel "outside" of their get together?

This last point is *very* important. Feeling on the outside looking in is one of the clearest identifiers of rejection. You often feel excluded from groups. You see people or groups as being close to one another, but you feel distant from those friends or acquaintances. The cycle of warfare I often see looks like this:

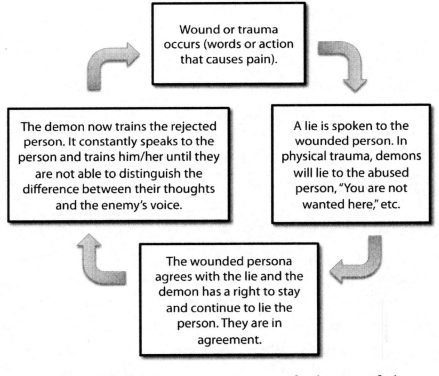

Wound or trauma occurs (words or action that causes pain).

A lie is spoken to the wounded person. In physical trauma, demons will lie to the abused person, "You are not wanted here," etc.

The wounded persona agrees with the lie and the demon has a right to stay and continue to lie the person. They are in agreement.

The demon now trains the rejected person. It constantly speaks to the person and trains him/her until they are not able to distinguish the difference between their thoughts and the enemy's voice.

Remember, the demonic presence is noted when our feelings are *out of control*, when we just can't seem to reign in our thoughts, fears, and worries about rejection, fear of rejection, or fear of failure. When interacting with those whom you want to accept you, you can often go into a slump, feeling sad, angry, depressed, and sullen because they don't receive and acknowledge you. *They can even do nothing but you feel rejected.* That is when we note that we might have allowed a spirit to hold on to us and we then need to expel it or have someone expel it.

These are possible signs that a demon of rejection is whispering lies to your heart and that you are *believing* and *accepting* those lies. The *degree* of your struggle indicates whether it is occasional harassment or demonic oppression.

Note that some of the above symptoms are because of other spirits that come in and work with rejection, such as spirits of self-pity, depression, self-hatred, fear of rejection, and fear of failure. My book *Demons, Angels, and Deliverance* discusses how demons can work in groups, but for now we want to focus on how rejection works and what to do about it.

As we close out this chapter, here is a summary of what I believe are the most important truths to remember about spiritual warfare:

- Our warfare, or battle, is not against humans who reject us, but against evil (demons) in this world (see 2 Corinthians 10 and Ephesians 6).

- Humans reject us, but there is a force of evil behind much, if not all, that we endure. We must see this to put a proper perspective in our relationships with those who hurt us. (Daniel 9–10 gives us glimpses of spiritual battles.)

- How do we know the devil and demons are real? We can trust scripture, which points to satan as the ruler of this world (see 2 Corinthians 4:4).

- Demons take on the name of their torment and sin. Mute spirits, a spirit of infirmity (Luke 13), and a spirit of divination (Acts 16) are a few biblical examples.

- We can conclude, therefore, that there is a spirit of rejection and that it can work in us just like any other demon. There can also be a hierarchy of demons that work against us (see Matthew 12).

- We can open the door to demons through our sin, and demons can also torment us and enter into us via another person's sin against us (see John 9:2).

- All demons are subject to the name of Jesus, for He defeated all powers of evil (see Ephesians 1:20–21 and Colossians 2:15).

FOR YOUR PERSONAL JOURNEY

Key Concept:

Being rejected is spiritual warfare! Remember that rejection is what fills satan's heart now and it's the primary weapon he uses to separate you from God and others.

Questions:

- Rejection is a spirit that wars after you to lie to you. What are some of the lies it has told you?

- What other aspects of spiritual warfare has this chapter helped you see, either in your life or in humanity?

CHAPTER 4

REJECTION AND REBELLION

Amy was a nice sixteen-year-old girl by all outside observations. She did her homework, obeyed her parents, had friends at school and in the neighborhood, and she even went to church regularly. In fact, she was even an exemplary Sunday School student. What only a few people knew about Amy was that she had another life. Amy was spending time with boys who didn't go to church, who smoked, did drugs, and wanted Amy to do sexual things she knew were wrong. Her parents loved her as best they could and she knew God loved her, but she wanted the attention of this other crowd. She desperately wanted to impress them, to get them to like her, even if it meant violating her conscience. Amy was rebelling and she didn't even know why.

Deep inside Amy's heart, something was missing, something we all need and seldom get. Amy's whole life was one broken promise after another from the primary source of affirmation for young girls—her father. Every time she wanted to spend time with Daddy (and he promised he would), he seemed to find more work at the office or at home or gave his time to her brothers instead. Sometimes a fight between her mother and father would suspend the promised bike ride or walk to the park. Sometimes he was just too tired.

And one more thing really bothered Amy—her father was always busy at the church. Three nights a week, he was there with her other friends doing youth group activities, Bible studies, or counseling some "wayward" young person. He was an elder and an occasional substitute preacher for the pastor. He was a good man, but in her mind, he just didn't care about *her*. So Amy found someone who would. She found a boy, a not-so-nice but *very attentive* boy. And Amy, at seventeen, got pregnant. Amy's rejection got the best of her and turned into rebellion.

How did it happen? It happened with a few choice words from the enemy of her soul, a few words that "hit the spot," words from her bad boyfriend like, "I care more than your dad, that's why I am here and he isn't," or, "If those Christians are so great, why don't they stop talking bad about me and be a real friend," or, "Amy, I hear you complain every day about being neglected by your parents, so why don't we just elope?"

Sound far-fetched? It happens every day. We were made to need and crave love and acceptance, and if we don't get it one place, we will look for it in another. In fact, we *will* find it, even if it means hurting others and ourselves to get it.

Take Lenny and Barb, for instance, married twenty years with two lovely children and a good, respectable career for Lenny as the pastor of a community church in a small town. Everyone knew them, liked them, and admired them and their small church. That is why everyone was so shocked when Lenny had an affair, leaving Barb and the kids for another woman—at least everyone except Lenny.

You see, for over twenty years, Lenny could never, ever do anything right. Barb always found something, somewhere, somehow to criticize. It was his sermons, his weight, his dress, or even his choice of words. Lenny, in his mind, was an abject failure and it grew heavier and heavier on him day after month after year after decade, until he found his remedy. One of his congregants, a divorced woman Lenny's age, thought Lenny was the most wonderful, bright, funny, and articulate man she had ever met, and she let him know it every chance she could. She didn't set out to steal Lenny, but she didn't have to.

Lenny ran into the arms of acceptance and out of the arms of rejection and failure. He rebelled all right, right down to the core of his being, right against everything he had ever lived for. But his need for acceptance and the rejection from his wife were stronger than his conscience. It was his mother and his girlfriends all rolled into one. Every failure in school replayed on video every time Barb told him to eat his food right or to clean up his car or how sloppy his sermons were.

Lenny didn't even know he was experiencing rejection until unconditional love and acceptance came knocking at his door. He just thought his life was how it was meant to be. But the enemy of his soul who knew his weakness waited and watched as his wife beat him down. He then moved in for the rebellion kill and Lenny's whole life went down the drain. Sound far-fetched again? It happens every day, and maybe, in some way, it's happened to you.

You have just read two fictitious accounts of how rejection can cause us to rebel against what we know to be right. The truth is that, for many of us, these accounts strike similarities to our own lives. The two characters, Amy and Lenny, both wanted love but never got it. They rebelled in order to get it. *But that is just the beginning of the cycle.* Let me give you another observation that is something I have learned over the years. Someone with a spirit of rejection in their life will, by the influence of that spirit, do rebellious, sinful acts almost unwittingly with the result that people further reject them (i.e. some attention is better than none), causing a vicious cycle

> **The spirit of rejection will cause you to do things that will cause more and more rejection!**

of rebellion-rejection-rebellion-rejection and on and on. You see, the spirit of rejection will cause you to do things that will cause more and more rejection!

This is the classic alcoholic/drug addict lifestyle—they do things that hurt loved ones and themselves, making people around them generally mad at them, yet in their heart, they need the love of the ones they are driving away. Their rebellion is getting people to reject them. This is the work of the *spirit of rejection.*

This was the life of my alcoholic mother and it also began to manifest in my daughter. Both were doing things that made you so mad you could scream, yet they both really wanted and needed love so desperately. Yet it is often very difficult to love someone who is being so obnoxious, rebellious, and hurtful! Do you know someone like that? Could this be who you really are today?

That is why I have made sure to include a section on spirits and spiritual warfare in this book. A *spirit* of rejection is real and when spirits drive us, we rarely are aware of the spiritual warfare that is involved. We can't see it and need others around us who are knowledgeable enough of the spirit world to help us. A simple way people have stated this concept is: rejected people reject others. Some, therefore, are stating that the rebellion we see in people's lives are their way of rejecting others before they get a chance to reject them. I am not sure that is always the case but I have met many people who operate this way.

Love Backwards

If I were to make the statement that most people who are wounded from rejection sin because they are insecure and want approval from those around them, you might think I am simpleminded and naïve. However, in the above scenarios I provided, the characters certainly rebelled against God and man, hurting both. They rebelled, as we all often do, because the pain of rejection was worse in their minds than the pain to themselves or loved ones that their rebellion would cause.

Many people abuse chemicals to dull the pain of rejection. After all, the desire for love is the most powerful desire in our lives and we were made to get it met. So when we don't get it in a healthy way, we will look for it elsewhere. But when we not only miss out on healthy love but also get the opposite—rejection—we will run to find something to ease the pain.

Now, perhaps you would say that many people sin, or rebel against what they know is best, simply to please themselves. I would agree that there are mixed motives when we disobey our conscience, but in twenty-five years as a Christian and with many years of praying with people and observing their behavior, I still maintain that we sin more often than not to get approval from others and to cover our insecurities.

Remember, when we feel rejected by parents, coaches, teachers, or even God Himself, we often say in our hearts, as Eve did, "I'll show you," or, "I'll get even." We often desire to impress those around us to get their love and affirmation because we didn't get it at home. We, in essence, try to take control of a life that feels out of control. When rejected by a loved one, the comfort and security we thought that we had in that relationship is weakened and thus breeds an immediate insecurity. Our natural response is to then strengthen our lives, so to speak, by taking control. That is why the most insecure and hurt people are also the most controlling.

> We sin more often than not to get approval from others and to cover our insecurities.

Let me outline some of life's "sin scenarios" and see if you can see how rejection can play a part:

- When we were young, how many of us drank either underage or too much to impress our friends?
- How many of us lie to feel a part of a group, such as our coworkers or boss?

- How many girls compromised their morals and became promiscuous because they wanted their date to like them and ask them out again?

- How many of us steal because we're insecure about our income and what it can really afford us?

- How many of us live beyond our means to "keep up with the Joneses"?

- How many times have we ignored God's convictions on our hearts because we thought He would punish us if we confessed who we really were (as if He didn't know)?

- How many times have we given "evangel-astic testimonies" (another term for a lie) to impress our friends?

- How many times have we just violated our conscience to get someone's approval?

The list goes on and on and, while not all sin has a fear of rejection at its root, much sin in our lives does have rejection at the root. The real question is: How would we behave if we had absolute security in God's love for us? What about if we felt secure in God's provision? God's acceptance? Or a loved one's acceptance?

Would we act in an entirely different manner if we knew no man or woman would or could reject us? The startling secret is—if you understand that you are a spirit being made by and for God—you would know that *no human can* truly reject you. What I mean is, since God made you and you exist for Him and He loves you entirely just the way you are today, then who can really reject you? Or does it matter if mere man rejects you if God loves you?

Paul the apostle said it this way, "If God is for us who can be against us?" (Romans 8:31). The answer is, of course, no one! Or more precisely, no human! The truth remains that most sin can be traced to rejection, and just as sin is spiritual, so is rejection—specifically, it is possible for a spirit of rejection to be present in our lives, influencing us and even controlling us. You will see this idea first introduced way back in Genesis when we see one of the first recorded examples of rejection. God *personifies sin* when He notes that Cain felt rejected by God.

The Bible has much to say about the spirit world that is worth learning. When it comes to rejection, no book ever written so openly shows men and women being rejected and the consequences of that rejection. How people responded in the Bible to rejection should be our greatest teacher on the subject.

You may know the story of Cain and his brother, Abel. Well, Cain felt rejected and then angry. Anger quickly follows rejection and then, if we bury it, depression will often set in. If you Google "anger and depression," you will find almost *eleven million* hits! The two are very much linked.

From Rejection to Murder?

In Genesis 4, we read the story of two brothers—Cain and his younger brother, Abel. Anyone who has had a sibling knows how the devil can pit one against the other. Satan is called "accuser of the brethren" for a reason. Read the passage as follows in the New Century Translation:

> Adam had sexual relations with his wife Eve, and she became pregnant and gave birth to Cain. Eve said, "With the Lord's help, I have given birth to a man." After that, Eve gave birth to Cain's brother Abel. Abel took care of flocks, and Cain became a farmer.
>
> Later, Cain brought some food from the ground as a gift to God. Abel brought the best parts from some of the firstborn of his flock. The Lord accepted Abel and his gift, **but he did not accept Cain and his gift. So Cain became very angry and felt rejected.**

The Lord asked Cain, "Why are you angry? Why do you look so unhappy? If you do things well, I will accept you, but if you do not do them well, sin is ready to attack you. Sin wants you, but you must rule over it."

Cain said to his brother Abel, "Let's go out into the field." While they were out in the field, Cain attacked his brother Abel and killed him.

The response of Cain is a classic rejection response: anger and hatred towards his fellow man, along with depression. Note that it says in most translations in verse 5, "Now Cain became very angry *and* his countenance fell." That "countenance fell" phrase is interesting because you can often see anger and depression on people's faces! It's hard to hide rejection and the Bible points that out.

There are several translations that say, "He became very angry and *felt rejected*." Note the relationship between the two here and that it says he *felt* rejected; it doesn't say God rejected him. God rejected the gift *not* the giver!

Now Abel did nothing to provoke Cain, but make no mistake, satan whispered in his ear that Abel was the source of his pain. I am sure Cain felt rejected by God. It says clearly that God *did not* accept Cain's gift. But don't forget that God spoke immediately to Cain to help him. He says, "*If* you do things well, *I will accept you.*"

The Injustice of Rejection

You can bet the devil told Cain that if he could get rid of that little brother, things between him and God would be fine. Can you just hear Cain saying, "Abel is God's little pet, always bringing those 'better' offerings!" Isn't that the way it always works? We get our anger focused on the wrong person or issue? The satanic response to rejection is to reject others, particularly the one we *think or feel* hurt us. But God always gives us a way out, a plan of action to redeem ourselves and forgive those who hurt us.

> No temptation has overtaken you except such as is common to man; but God is faithful, who will not allow you to be tempted beyond what you are able, but with the temptation will also make the way of escape, that you may be able to bear it. —1 Corinthians 10:13

When we are rejected or feel rejected, we can turn to God for an answer. In Cain's situation, God told him to "continue to do well" to be accepted. The very fact that God saw his feelings of rejection and then spoke to him should have given Cain great confidence.

> The satanic response to rejection is to reject others, particularly the one we *think or feel* hurt us.

God showed that He knew Cain's heart and that He cared for him. God gave him a way out. Cain, on the other hand, turned to another classic response of rejection—anger and revenge. Cain immediately proved Jesus' statement in Matthew 5 that hatred in our hearts is the same as murder, simply because you can't have murder without first having hatred.

> You have heard that it was said to those of old, "You shall not murder; and whoever murders will be liable to judgment." But I say to you that everyone who is angry with his brother will be liable to judgment; whoever insults his brother will be liable to the council; and whoever says, "You fool!" will be liable to the hell of fire. So if you are offering your gift at the altar and there remember that your brother has something against you, leave your gift there before the altar and go. First be reconciled to your brother, and then come and offer your gift. Come to terms quickly with your accuser while you are

going with him to court, lest your accuser hand you over to the judge, and the judge to the guard, and you be put in prison. Truly, I say to you, you will never get out until you have paid the last penny. —Matthew 5:21–26

Jesus makes a clear correlation between anger and murder, and of course we know that Cain is a primary example. When we feel rejected as Cain did, it is important to recognize what we are saying to ourselves or what the enemy of our souls is whispering to us in some way. The message we often receive is, "I've been wronged and there is an *injustice here.*"

God made humans with a moral code and that moral code always wants to right the wrongs and fix the injustices in the world. We feel emotionally, morally, and spiritually out of balance or lop-sided. So if we have had an injustice done to us, what is our normal response? We must correct it. But of course, we often do it without God, in our own time and manner, and without His blessing.

> We can't avoid rejection and disappointment in life, but we can avoid the rebellion and anger to which it leads.

Behind almost all anger is someone who carries an injustice done to them. If you've been molested, abused, cheated, stolen from, or otherwise wronged in life, you will carry anger in your heart from these rejections unless you were able to give it to God and not take it personally. Most of us are unaware of this. It is only when we are secure in the Father's love that we can release anger and give it to God. Why else would we be reminded in scripture, "Vengeance is Mine, and I will repay" (Hebrews 10:30)? If we remind ourselves of Cain's example, we'll see that God knew ahead of time what Cain's reaction would be and prepared a remedy. It's the same for you and me! We can't avoid rejection and disappointment in life, but we can avoid the rebellion and anger to which it leads.

Rejection Doesn't Have to Win

God continued to show His love and concern for Cain by not only giving him instructions to keep in good standing with Him, but the Lord warned him that sin (satan) was stalking him, that it was personal, and "its desire is for you" (Genesis 4:5). Now also notice that God told Cain that he must "rule over it." This means that Cain *could have ruled over sin*! God cannot ask us to do something we cannot do. To do so would be unjust.

This tells me that there is no rejection that God cannot give us victory over! I don't know what hurts you have experienced, but can you imagine the very God of glory rejecting your offering? Can you imagine knowing that the God who created you has now rejected your work? Before we judge Cain too harshly, let us remember what he endured. Cain *did* experience a form of rejection, but make no mistake, God was right there to help him through it. God was near to you when you experienced your moments of rejection too, but the question is, did you turn to Him or did you take matters in your own hands? Did you curse those who hurt you? Did you condemn them and dismiss them? Note Jesus' response as written by an eyewitness of His moment of rejection.

> Christ also suffered for us, **leaving us an example**, that you should follow His steps: "Who committed no sin, nor was deceit found in His mouth"; who, **when He was reviled, did not revile in return**; when He suffered, He did not threaten, **but committed Himself to Him who judges righteously**.
>
> —1 Peter 2:21–23

Jesus gives us the right response to rejection. Cain's example is given immediately in scripture as a precursor of what man is capable of if he does not turn to God to solve his problems. We either take our own vengeance, as Cain did by killing his brother, or we do what Jesus did and "trust Him who judges righteously." There are only two paths to resolve our hurts. Now you may not have killed your rejecter, but you may carry hatred instead, which Jesus warned us is on the same plane as murder.

Now you may suppose that this whole event with Cain and Abel was a test, and that is a possibility. But the key to this passage is not in the test but in the response. Whether it was a test or not, God says Cain could have passed that test by telling him that he could rule over the sin of revenge.

Here is an example of the cycle most rejection takes:

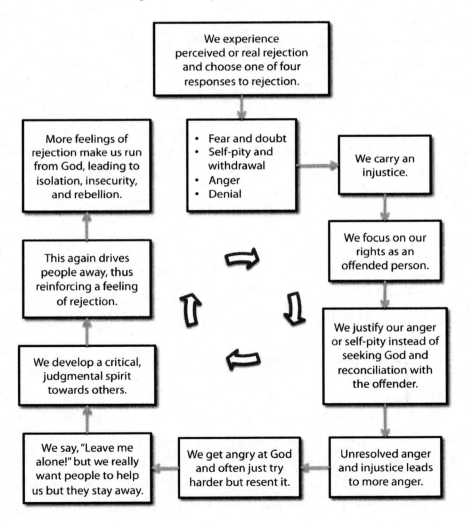

The above scenario has many variables and it cannot be a rule to judge all situations. But it is the most common cycle I have found and I believe it warrants our attention when we start sliding into feelings of resentment and anger because of rejection.

We can learn the following from Cain and Abel:

- When we feel rejected, we have a feeling of an injustice done to us.
- This injustice makes us feel out of balance and thus we want to "right the ship" and get some type of vengeance.
- Anger will then be carried in our hearts, poisoning us.
- If we don't give it to God, sin and rebellion will stalk us (there is a person(ality) behind temptation).
- We can, however, master that personality or temptation by listening to God's voice. But if we do not, then…
- We can begin to believe satan's greatest and most important lie—that *God* has rejected us.
- Thus, if God has rejected us, then why turn to Him for help? We then turn to the world system for comfort, which always leads to lust for things, or envy and hatred of others, and in the end, rebellion towards God.

God In the Midst of It

I remember when I began to get healing from being molested as a young boy. The Lord began to show me pictures of the incident and some of the fear it led to in my life. But at the same time, I began to see Him there in those incidents holding me and covering me even as I was abused. I knew He was there for me, even as God was conscious of Cain's feelings of rejection and anger. Yes, the Lord knew my fear, confusion, and anger. At one point, I heard Him speak to me during one of these flashbacks. He said, "I'll make this right." Then He quickened to my mind the verse I quoted earlier: "Vengeance is mine and I will repay." That doesn't always mean that He will kill, destroy, or hurt the abusers in our lives. In fact, their sin and all sin always carries its own punishment and pain. But beyond that, God deals with people even in this life to make things right. Jesus spoke to this when He talked about generational judgment falling on those who didn't receive His message (see Matthew 23:30–35).

This "vengeance" actually might not look like what we would think. In fact, in my case, I was able to lead my abusers to the Lord! But the way God "made it right" in my life was by preventing even more emotional damage than I might have had from six-plus years of abuse. He saved me at eighteen years of age and subsequently continued to nurture me in the faith so I could get healing. He will do the same for you!

For Your Personal Journey

Key Concept:

> There is a direct correlation between rejection and rebellion. When we are hurt, we have a sense of injustice and we take it upon ourselves to make things right. This often takes the form of revenge, which is taking back something that you feel has been taken away.

Questions:

- What rebellion/sin is working in your life that is tied to rejection or a sense of being hurt?
- Is there anger in your life that is tied to rejection (like Cain)?

CHAPTER 5

REJECTION AND SELF-PITY

I n the previous chapter, we looked at Cain's response to his rejection incident and focused on the anger and rebellion it lead to. Here I want to examine another aspect that God wants to point out for all us. Keep in mind that the Bible is a book of thousands of years of history that God not only inspired, but also had to compact into a very portable book. That means He didn't waste one word. So in Genesis 4:5, it says that "Cain became very angry," *and* that his "countenance fell." Let's look at some other translations of that verse and focus on another phase of rejection—depression and/or self-pity:

> But did not accept Kayin and his offering. Kayin was very angry, and **his face fell.** —CJB
>
> So Cain became very angry and was **disappointed.** —GW
>
> Cain became furious, and he **scowled in anger.** —GNT
>
> Cain was furious, and he was **downcast.** —HCSB
>
> And Cain was angry and **his face became sad.** —BBE

This made Cain very angry and **dejected.** —NLT

Cain lost his temper and **went into a sulk.** —MSG

It is very interesting and revealing that God chose not only to point out the anger that led to Abel's murder, but also another aspect of Cain's reaction to God's perceived rejection of himself and his offering. The fact that Cain was angry is something we can relate to, but what is sometimes less noticeable to those around us are those who quietly become sad and sulk away instead of openly displaying anger when they feel rejected. I can pretty much imagine that Cain didn't yell at God, scream, or throw fits, openly showing his anger. The scripture is clear that he was "very angry," but the *only* outward, physical sign was that his "face fell." The NLT says he was "dejected," while another says, "downcast." Well, it wasn't just his face, but his whole being was "sulking"; it's just that it was seen on his face.

> Self-pity can lead to murder or a life of bitterness in your heart. We know medically that unresolved bitterness can actually kill.

I find The Message translation of particular interest here because it says he "went into a sulk." Many parents of toddlers and young adults have seen this. The child knows he or she cannot defy you outright and take over so he or she slips into a pouty attitude. They sulk away, go to their room, and shut down, usually hoping to be followed after by the parent with some bargaining soon to take place! I've been there, done that one!

I remember that my son Zachary at about three or so began the classic inverted smile when he didn't get his way. It was cute, but of course he was not able to hide his disappointment. As adults, when we get older, we know how to hide our feelings from those around us. But God never misses a thing.

Some parents chase children to fix these problems and some leave them alone. I won't get into a parenting lesson here, but we can see the self-pity on the face of the rejected one. Left unchecked and unresolved, it can be as deadly as Cain's. It can lead to murder or a life of bitterness in their hearts. We know medically that unresolved bitterness can actually kill. It leads to autoimmune disorders that eat at the body. I believe cancer, fibromyalgia, arthritis, and many other diseases come from bitterness, which comes from unresolved rejections.

The Voice of Rejection

Because there is a real, spiritual enemy behind sin and its temptations, I want to point out to you a very, very important concept. I say it this way: *rejection speaks*! I mean that once we give in to the spiritual forces of sin, it speaks to our hearts to tempt, seduce, and otherwise lead us astray. That is why Israel, God's first people, was warned to constantly look at, study, and teach the Word of God to their people, both young and old, even to the point of wearing it on their clothes!

If you only listen to the voice of rejection, you will give in to anger, self-pity, lust, control, and more. Rejection will become rebellion. The Bible talks about another voice that guides us in addition to the voice of the Lord directly—the voice of scripture.

> My son, keep your father's commandment, and forsake not your mother's teaching. Bind them on your heart always; tie them around your neck. When you walk, they will lead you; when you lie down, they will watch over you; and when you awake, they will talk with you. —Proverbs 6:20–22

What will you do when rejection whispers in your ear, "Hey, God doesn't love you; look at your life, it stinks! Why not go ahead and get drunk tonight or _____ (fill in the blank and pick your sin)"? Will there be another voice to keep you from sin?

Again, let's remind ourselves that God notes the personality of sin crouching at Cain's door to tempt him the very moment he felt rejected by God! Yes, rejection speaks! But so does scripture! God has good things to say to us to counter-balance, if you will, the voice of the enemy. The question is, can you hear the good voice? Many of us still can't, so we need others outside our situation to speak the truth to us.

These spiritual forces speak to us, but they also filter what we hear or focus on. If you read Genesis 4 again and note how God warned Cain, you'll see something very interesting. Cain seemed to *forget the promise* part of God's words to him after God did not accept his offering. It was as if he missed the good part of what God said. Do you remember it? "But *if you do well* will not your countenance be lifted up?" (Genesis 4:7). That's a rhetorical question because of course God will accept Him and "lift up his countenance," which is the Hebrew way of saying, "to make happy or accepted."

> ⤳
>
> **The unredeemed mind is self-focused and will not listen to the voice of love and the promises of God, but rather on what is *not* happening.**

Other translations say:

> **You will be accepted if you respond in the right way**. But if you refuse to respond correctly, then watch out! Sin is waiting to attack and destroy you, and you must subdue it. — NLT

> If you do things well, **I will accept you**, but if you do not do them well, sin is ready to attack you. Sin wants you, but you must rule over him. —NCV

Here God promised to lift up Cain if he did well and offered a new and better sacrifice like Abel's, but Cain only focused on the fact that God didn't like the first go around. I deal with that all the time as a parent. If I tell one of my children, "No, you can't have a treat right now, but after dinner you'll get a big bowl of ice cream," what do you think they focus on? That's right, they focus on that they don't get a treat right when they wanted it!

The unredeemed mind is self-focused and will not listen to the voice of love and the promises of God, but rather on what is *not* happening. It's the glass half-full scenario. The only problem is that a lifestyle of this leads to depression, self-pity, anger, jealousy, lust, and a whole host of things that make for one unhappy person.

That spirit of rejection will speak to you and tell you, "You've been cheated again, life stinks, and it's not fair." If you listen to it, you'll end up with anger and hatred, even toward God. After all, He's in charge right?

> Rejection mutes and rejection speaks. It won't let you hear the good that God's Word offers you, but it shouts about the bad that has happened to you.

Rejection will not only focus on what you did wrong, but it will filter or keep you from hearing what *God's solution* can be to all of your problems. So perhaps we could say that rejection mutes and rejection speaks. It won't let you hear the good that God's Word offers you, but it shouts about the bad that has happened to you. I will not deny that you may have had many great and evil injustices done to you as did I during my childhood years. But like Cain, God provided me with a way of escape, healing, and wholeness through Jesus and His suffering in my place on the cross.

Ahab and the Grapes of (Jezebel's) Wrath

Let us look at a classic case of perceived rejection and how the spirit of self-pity works with it. Read 1 Kings 21–22 to familiarize yourself with King Ahab and his adventure with Naboth, Naboth's vineyard, and his "lovely" wife, Queen Jezebel. But here is the first key part of the story:

> Now it came about after these things that Naboth the Jezreelite had a vineyard, which was in Jezreel beside the palace of Ahab king of Samaria. Ahab spoke to Naboth, saying, "Give me your vineyard, that I may have it for a vegetable garden because it is close beside my house, and I will give you a better vineyard than it in its place; if you like, I will give you the price of it in money." But Naboth said to Ahab, "The LORD forbid me that I should give you the inheritance of my fathers." So Ahab came into his house sullen and vexed because of the word which Naboth the Jezreelite had spoken to him; for he said, "I will not give you the inheritance of my fathers." And he lay down on his bed and turned away his face and ate no food. But Jezebel his wife came to him and said to him, "How is it that your spirit is so sullen that you are not eating food?" So he said to her, "Because I spoke to Naboth the Jezreelite and said to him, 'Give me your vineyard for money; or else, if it pleases you, I will give you a vineyard in its place.' But he said, 'I will not give you my vineyard.'" Jezebel his wife said to him, "Do you now reign over Israel? Arise, eat bread, and let your heart be joyful; I will give you the vineyard of Naboth the Jezreelite." So she wrote letters in Ahab's name and sealed them with his seal, and sent letters to the elders and to the nobles who were living with Naboth in his city. Now she wrote in the letters, saying, "Proclaim a fast and seat Naboth at the head of the people; and seat two worthless men before him, and let them testify against him, saying, 'You cursed God and the king.' Then take him out and stone him to death."

King Ahab wanted his neighbor Naboth's vineyard and when he didn't get his way, he went "into his house sullen and vexed." The American Heritage Dictionary defines *sullen* as "brooding, lethargic or slow, *resentful*, *gloomy*, alone, morose."[6] This same dictionary defines *vexed* as "annoyed with petty importunities, *agitated* "[7] (emphasis mine in both definitions). Does any of this sound familiar to you? I know I have brooded when I didn't get my way. I would be gloomy, *hoping someone would notice me.* I was trying to draw them into my pit of depression and get them to say, "What's wrong, sweetie? What can I get you? How can I soothe you?" On and on the game of manipulation goes. We've all done it!

Now, in some situations, like a parent to a child who has been truly wronged by another, this might be appropriate. But as adults, we often use the perceived injustice to get a human solution to something God should be involved with. We often use rejection to manipulate others. But the sad part is that man can never fully heal our wounds, which is why we have a loving Father who is called "the Father of [all] spirits" (Hebrews 12:9). Rejection is spiritual and it needs a spiritual response.

So, basically, Ahab pouted like a little baby. Indeed, I am sure he felt rejected. The devil probably came along and whispered, "Some king you are! You can't even get some subject of yours to give you a vineyard when you offer to pay him," or, "What kind of man are you to be refused by this weasel, Naboth?"

> We often use rejection to manipulate others. But we can never fully heal our wounds. Rejection is spiritual and it needs a spiritual response.

Remember that I mentioned there are three responses to rejection that I outlined in chapter one? This is number three—withdrawal, depression, and self-pity. The sneaky part here is that satan will often appeal to your pride when this happens. The hard part is that when you meet people who are depressed, you rarely think they have a problem with pride, but they often do. It's just masked by an apparent victim mentality because they seem so wounded.

Withdrawal

Notice verse four in the passage about Ahab. It says he "turned his face away." One of the most classics signs of a root of rejection is hiding, withdrawal, quitting, running away. That's what Adam and Eve did after they sinned; that's what Cain did when he felt rejected by God; and of course it's what Ahab did.

We run away from what we don't like, do we not? I admit sometimes going away is not a bad solution, like in the midst of a heated argument. But most times when we run away it's an unhealthy response to rejection. Like Ahab, it can turn into manipulation. I too used to withdraw from people when rejection ran my life.

But in truth I didn't want to go away, not deep, deep down. I wanted love, affection, and affirmation—all the things I didn't get as a child. But rejection drove me away, unwittingly. That's what spirits do; they drive us. Are they driving you to go away or withdraw too? We need to know how we respond to rejection. If we discover that, we'll find the pain places in our lives.

I compare rejection to a thumb that's been smacked by a hammer. That thumb is sore, red, and throbbing. So when someone bumps it, we jerk back in pain. We withdraw that thumb from being touched. So it is with our sore, throbbing hearts. Rejection was the hammer that smacked our hearts and now when we're "bumped" by more rejection, we pull away. Sometimes withdrawing is good for a season or short time. But eventually you and I have to confront our fears and rejection and actually seek out God and others to bandage that thumb of our hearts and get healed.

When you are reacting to rejection by "turning your face away" as Ahab did, you are embracing one of two mind-sets:

- You are testing those around you. You want to see if they care enough to pursue you. But when they do, because pride usually sneaks in and says you don't need them because it's a cove for insecurity, you tell the pursuer to go away.

- You are fearful of your capacity. You feel overwhelmed by the rejection/pain of something or someone. You have no room left in your heart for more rejection and so you run. But here is the truth. The only way to increase your (spiritual-emotional) capacity is by communication. Communication increases the capacity of your heart and defeats rejection!

Why do you think David had such a heart for God? Because he spoke to God, prayed to God, sang to God, and cried out to God more than anyone in the Bible. He is called "a man after God's own heart" in Acts 2:32 because he had a large heart and thus capacity for God.

> The only way to increase your (spiritual-emotional) capacity is by communication. Communication increases the capacity of your heart and defeats rejection!

So the next time you find yourself running away, ask yourself, "Do I really want to have someone show me love?" or "Am I really feeling overwhelmed (out of capacity) because I haven't communicated?"

Listen to the self-talk in your heart and pay attention to the spirit behind your words. Then you'll know where your rejection is pointing the loaded gun. Of course your reaction to rejection might indeed be different. But I use Ahab to point out how some may react to rejection.

When you feel like running away from an argument, rejection, pain, tension, etc., tell yourself it is the spirit of rejection that is driving you and go in the opposite direction—spiritually, emotionally, and yes, physically.

Remember, withdrawal and going away never heals your rejection; it just prolongs the healing process. Also, you can withdraw and run away in your heart and emotions and try to cover it up so no one sees. Some physically go away and others emotionally go away, but neither is healthy long term. Hiding feels good but it will almost always turn to anger and depression.

Make sure that you are aware of emotional withdrawal as much as physical withdrawal. This is going to be difficult because as one who withdraws you believe it is your safe spot. It's like Elijah running in the cave. By the way, he got into self-pity and withdrawal too! But remember, God met Elijah in his cave and He'll meet you in your cave. But you must be willing as Elijah was to listen to God in the midst of your hiding.

Misery Loves (Ungodly) Company

We won't get into a study of the spirit of Jezebel here, but I wanted to point out how we can involve others in our sin when we feel rejected. This is especially true when the spirit of self-pity is at work as it was here with "poor Ahab." When men have women in their lives who are ungodly and they get under self-pity, the men will become sluggish, lethargic, and lose their drive to deal with life. This opens the door for this spirit, through the woman, to take the bull by the horns as Jezebel did in verse six when she said, "I will give you the vineyard of Naboth."

"Wow, things are looking up," Ahab must have thought. "I'll just let my wife get what I want for me. Perhaps this sulking and pouting things works pretty good!" People learn how to use self-pity to their advantage very early in life. Make no mistake; it's a powerful tool. No one likes to see a loved one cry or suffer.

But when self-pity comes from rejection and it gets a hold on a man, it makes the man a wimp, period. I have experienced it personally and seen it many times in others. It can also work on women who then give in to a controlling and abusive man in their life. In either case, *without* knowing the Lord's love for us, rejection—be it perceived, as in Ahab's case, or real—can lead to self-pity and many other demonic problems. Ahab chose to manipulate those around him to do his bidding.

There is always a potential for right and wrong responses to rejection. Until you practice the healing steps in this book or get other similar help, you will continue to let past rejection pervert your relationships and future rejection will have too much power over you. Self-pity is the sneakiest of the results of rejection because it seems so natural; after all, we were hurt, weren't we?

> Self-pity is the sneakiest of the results of rejection because it seems so natural; after all, we were hurt, weren't we?

Now I want you to remember our old friend King Saul and see that this self-pity is common among even leaders! King Ahab was not alone in his whining and self-pity response to not getting what he wanted. I have even wondered if this type of self-pity is even worse for those who are leaders. When Saul was chasing David in the wilderness and it seemed that he could even bribe the sons of Benjamin, he said this:

"(Is) there none of you who is sorry for me…"

—1 Samuel 22:8, 9

Can you imagine a leader of a country saying this? It would seem sick and sad. So Ahab is not an isolated case but rather a symptom perhaps of those who are used to getting their way, and when they get rejected, or *perceive* rejection, they really have a hard time with it. In my mind many Americans are like Ahab, spoiled and used to getting their way and they feel very rejected when things don't work out. Whether it's real rejection or not, the result can be the same: self-pity, lethargy, and spiritual apathy.

Unresolved Rejection Makes Us Weak

You might say about Queen Jezebel, "Wasn't she a loving wife just trying to help her hubby?" No, she was someone usurping authority and getting out of God's pattern. How do I know? Look at the fruit—lying, conniving, and murder. You can see from God's response that He wasn't too happy. Look at these verses:

> So Ahab said to Elijah, "Have you found me, O my enemy?" And he answered, "I have found you, because you have **sold yourself to do evil in the sight of the Lord.** Behold, I will bring calamity on you. I will take away your posterity, and will cut off from Ahab every male in Israel, both bond and free. I will make your house like the house of Jeroboam the son of Nebat, and like the house of Baasha the son of Ahijah, because of the provocation with which you have provoked Me to anger, and made Israel sin." …But there **was no one like Ahab** who **sold himself** to do wickedness in the sight of the Lord, **because Jezebel his wife stirred him up.**
>
> —1 Kings 21:20–22, 25

Did you see how God said to Ahab twice that he "sold himself to do wickedness"? What does that mean? It means he forgot his real identity and took a cheap substitute. To sell yourself means you don't know your real value, just as a prostitute sells herself to a man to be used of him because she doesn't know her real value as a woman and as a person. Remember how I said rejection steals from us? Remember how I noted that the worst thing it steals is God's real identity for you? Well, that is what Ahab allowed rejection to do to him.

He was a child of God, and a king at that! He could have bought any nice vineyard, but because he had some roots of rejection already working in his life, he turned to the quick, cheap, and whining route: whine and complain to the wife, look depressed, get into self-pity to see if someone else will help you. Instead, he should have prayed and sought God and perhaps even God would have convinced Naboth to sell him the vineyard for a good price and they both would have won!

Think about how you might have used self-pity, depression, whining, or moping around to get your way. We all do it, but we do it because we don't know *who* we are. Whether you are a Christian or not, God has a great love for you and loves you more than you can possibly imagine. After all, look at the cross of Christ. God did that because He loved you. But if you are a Christian, you are now a real child of God, and the Father of Glory is your own Daddy. You have a new identity of greatness. You are most loved and favored and scripture says, "If any man is in Christ he is a new creation, all things are become new!" (2 Corinthians 5:17).

> Think about how you might have used self-pity, depression, whining, or moping around to get your way. We all do it, but we do it because we don't know *who* we are.

Now back to Ahab. God gave some harsh judgments to Ahab, no? God promised to cut off all his descendants, send calamity, and more. God even said that Ahab "made Israel sin." So a whole nation was led into sin because of this ungodly king and his response to rejection. That is what was said of Jezebel his wife, as the same spirit that worked in her in Ahab's day came back thousands of years later in Revelation 2:20.

Revelation 2 says that this spirit/person, Jezebel, was leading people, even leaders in a church, into sin! It was attracted to leaders, kings, and others in authority. You will see this spirit today in the church find a person of influence (mostly men) and manipulate them just like she did to Ahab. Why? Because he made a place for her by responding to rejection with weakness, self pity, and lethargy. And you should also note that even first century Christian men had done the *same thing* as Ahab—they tolerated her conniving.

Basically, Ahab gave up his drive, authority, and leadership because he felt sorry for himself for not getting his way. He allowed rejection to rule. Instead of turning to the Lord and becoming *thankful and grateful* that he was king and had a whole palace, he whined about not getting a little vineyard! The key truth to remember here is that thankfulness is one of the most powerful tools against rejection.

> ~
> **Thankfulness is one of the most powerful tools against rejection.**

Note that God's statement in His judgment towards Ahab was that he allowed Jezebel to "stir him up." What does that mean? It means she influenced him in a negative way or pushed him to the point of a king acquiescing to a queen. Women have an incredible ability to influence, and trust me, it is no less powerful in the life of a public leader. Ahab allowed or enabled his wife Jezebel to murder Naboth and thus deepened his sin before God. Ahab clearly couldn't handle the rejection he got from Naboth, so he turned to rebellion. He rebelled against God by not using his authority as a husband and king to say no to Jezebel's plot to kill Naboth. You might say that he started out in the sin of covetousness, which is true, but my point is *how he dealt with not getting his lust fulfilled.* He allowed rejection to come in and then put others up to do his dirty work, to fulfill his lust. Ahab let rejection lead to rebellion in the worst way.

Lust and Rejection

You should note the relationship with weak men, strong women, and lust. There was rejection in here on Ahab's part, make no mistake, but he lusted after Naboth's vineyard for sure and you can bet he had a problem with lust and it was misused in his relationship with Jezebel. One doesn't have to be too astute to guess that Jezebel had a problem with lust, especially lust for power. So when she is mentioned in Revelation 2:20 centuries later, she is connected with lust and leading people into (sexual) sin.

> ...**Jezebel,** who calls herself a prophetess, to teach and **seduce My servants to commit sexual immorality**.

When men are rejected, they become weak, and one of the first sins they will go into is sexual sin. They lose their ability to have discipline and self-control. But *why* are they weak in the first place? It is normally because rejection has caused them to see themselves as failed, flawed, unloved, and unwanted, and this has created an internal image of weakness and neediness. So where else would someone run to in order to find something that looks like love? Lust of course, since it is the cheap copy of love. Sexual intercourse is the highest form of bonding humans can experience, so people run to it when they don't have a real, loving marriage. Men in sexual bondage go to fornication (intercourse outside of marriage) because it forms a bond that feels like love.

Strong women dominate these kinds of men because they have a poor self-image, or what I prefer to call a poor "God-image"—God's image of them and their image of God! I have rarely met someone who struggled with lust who did not have a root of rejection in his or her life.

Perhaps this Jezebel–Ahab episode seems like such a drastic situation that you can't relate. Let me bring it to a more practical level. Perhaps you have been jealous of someone, or someone you know was promoted in some way ahead of you and you felt cheated or that things were unjust, so you began to gossip about that person to, in essence, murder them with your words. Remember, Jezebel had men bring false accusations against Naboth and then they had him stoned. We can do that with gossip, back biting, and unforgiveness. Perhaps it only went to the extent of evil thoughts in your heart and nothing more. Did you know that Jesus said that "evil thoughts" will "defile a man" (Mark 7:21–23)? Defilement here can be taken as in a sin that leads to damnation. Jezebel probably had a root of rejection as well. Rejected people are drawn to other rejected people and it makes for a very tough relationship.

More to the point, a heart full of rejection will not allow others to get ahead without feeling wounded, cheated, and personally hurt. It often partners with lust, sexual or otherwise, to get what it wants. Rejection says to its host, "You've been cheated and wounded, you poor thing; you deserve _____ (Naboth's vineyard, for example)." Whatever it is that you want, the "poor person" that rejection has made you out to be will speak to you in order to get you to take revenge or whatever it is that you want.

The "spirit" of Ahab

Whenever this portion of scripture in 1 Kings 21–22 is discussed, it invariably leads to a focus on Jezebel and her manipulations and the fact that she is mentioned in Revelation centuries later. But many people have also noticed that there can be a "spirit" of Ahab just as there seems to be a spirit of Jezebel that carried down through the centuries. I agree with the idea that a "spirit of Jezebel" exists because its behavior was almost identical to the action of the original queen in the Old Testament. As we'll see in the next chapter, demons take on the name of their activity and sometimes are so powerful and arrogant that they take on the name of a person.

If there is a "spirit" of Ahab, it isn't mentioned in the Bible, but that doesn't mean it doesn't exist. I would say that if one is led to pray against a spirit of Ahab, he is praying against a demon that causes the same sins as Ahab: self-pity, apathy, laziness, weakness, and spiritual lethargy, as well as manipulation. So though I don't normally address a spirit of Ahab, I wouldn't tell people it can't exist. The case for Jezebel seems to be stronger but I would agree that a "spirit" of Ahab might have provided a "place for" the spirit of Jezebel to exist. Ahab's self pity and apathy created a vacuum for his wicked wife to step into. So when one says, "He has a spirit of Ahab," I would remind myself of Ahab's sins and pray accordingly. The same would go for dealing with a spirit of Jezebel. Again, spiritual warfare and demonology will be discussed next.

In summary, we see that rejection, and self-pity, and withdrawal are companions. The self-pity and withdrawal response to rejection has the following patterns:

- Draws others into our dilemma.
- Lives in the past, rehearsing old injustices done.
- Causes spiritual weakness, lethargy, apathy, and laziness.
- Allows us to be controlled by others.
- Tries to control others as well, but in an underhanded manner.
- Leads to depression and hopelessness.
- Causes us to go away and sulk, and to be lonely (often with the express intent of actually drawing others to us without words; it's indirect and thus manipulative).
- Leads to just as much sin as the more overt anger that rejection can cause.

FOR YOUR PERSONAL JOURNEY

Key Concept:

Whether it's real or perceived rejection, we will easily feel sorry for ourselves if we don't focus on God's response to our situation. Watch out for self-pity because it will attract the wrong people and spirit(s)!

Questions:

- How have I allowed rejection to lead to self-pity? Depression?
- Do I consistently perceive rejection when I don't get my way and sulk as a result?

CHAPTER 6

REJECTION AND THE FEAR OF MAN

S o far we have learned that rejection can be a root or foundation
in our lives and rejection is usually the first negative emotion we
encounter. We've seen that there are four reactions to rejection:
doubt and fear, anger, withdrawal and self-pity, and denial. We studied
the first cases of (perceived) rejection in Adam and Eve and then their
first son Cain and saw the horrific consequences. We then learned that
there is a spirit world and that Lucifer/satan is the god of the dark side
of this world. Satan uses rejection as his main tactic to keep us from
God because he himself is full of rejection due to his rebellion that led
to his expulsion from heaven. We now move on to examine the work
of rejection in two kings—Saul and David—so we can learn from their
mistakes and successes.

Let's look at King Saul and his road to rebellion that came from
rejection. Like all roads, it was a process and it had some turns in it,

perhaps like your road. But we know what was at the *beginning* of his journey: rejection, or more specifically, *passive* rejection.

Quiet Shame

In 1 Samuel 10, Saul is *publicly chosen* as king and praised by the prophet Samuel as being a *good choice* for a king (10:23–25). Samuel even confirms that *God* has chosen Saul. This should have gone a long way into breaking off much of the root of rejection Saul may have experienced up to that point in life. Many times, if one has only minor experience with rejection, a life-changing event that affirms us will heal a wound (marriage, a promotion, a visitation from the Lord, etc.). These can all help heal *minor* rejection wounds. God really did a lot to affirm Saul. After all, Samuel said it was the "word of the Lord" to Saul (9:27). We have some history on Saul's childhood, but his adulthood reveals serious foundational problems.

> One of the two main sources of rejection *is other people's words.*

One of the most important points to notice here is the power of the spoken word. One of the two main sources of rejection *is other people's words.* Early on after Saul is proclaimed king, something happens that possibly shapes his whole future. He is criticized *publicly* and he does not even respond. Instead, he seems to take his accuser's words to heart. Note the following verse:

> Then Samuel explained to the people the behavior of royalty, and wrote it in a book and laid it up before the Lord. And Samuel sent all the people away, every man to his house. And Saul also went home to Gibeah; and valiant men went with him, whose hearts God had touched. But some rebels **said,** "How can this man save us?" **So they despised him,** and brought him no presents. **But he [Saul] held his peace.**
> —1 Samuel 10:25–27

I believe Saul's silence points to one of the main spirits that works with rejection: shame. Shame often causes us to withdraw, turn inward and live in the shadows. It will cause us to be silent, especially when we need to stand up for ourselves.

Rejected Son, Rejected King

Note here that he was "despised" by some around him. In fact, Saul must have heard these men talking about him because it says, "he held his peace." How many of us have been wounded by words and done nothing about it? If Saul would have immediately confronted those men, then he may have never allowed rejection and insecurity to take a hold on his life. But he didn't and thus, I believe, he suffered for it. I think his kingship got off to an insecure start and it led to a life of rebellion. Now we shall also see that Saul already had a root of rejection from his father. But this event, I believe, cemented it in and it was never broken.

This event was significant enough that it is brought up again in a later verse:

> Then the people said to Samuel, "Who is he who said, 'Shall Saul reign over us?' Bring the men, that we may put them to death." —1 Samuel 11:12

They could have by right put those who "despised him in their hearts" to death, but Saul spares them. Saul was officially king now and you didn't mock a king back then. This shows the severity of their mocking and its probable impact on Saul. But because Saul was already a rejected son, he was easily rejected as a king. When you carry rejection and shame in your heart, it is easy for people to reject you because they sense you don't value yourself, so why should they value you.

> Because Saul was already a rejected son, he was easily rejected as a king.

I want to mention again that I believe the impact of Saul's passive rejection from his father resulted in an overriding sense of shame. Shame often goes undetected because it causes people to be silent. Shame tells you that you have no right to stand up for yourself and take care of yourself. It makes you feel like you have no value and thus should take the abuse given to you. Rejection works with the spirit of shame to create a "package" of someone who will keep silent and just "bear up" under life. I believe that because Saul's father Kish was a "valiant warrior" (1 Kings 9:1). Saul felt shame for not being "like Dad." People probably constantly put huge expectations on him to follow in his dad's footsteps. When he didn't always measure up to the five generations of men listed in his family line in scripture, he felt worthless and shameful. This was the result of the rejection he experienced from a father who was too busy for him.

Good Beginnings, Bad Endings

After becoming king in 1 Samuel 10, Saul does go on to great military success. Spiritually, he also seems to start off well, being found among the prophets and was thus doubly honored. Finally, he is reconfirmed as king in chapter 11.

But starting in chapter 13, we see Saul's lack of trust in God and in His chosen voice to the people—Samuel the prophet. At this time in God's plan for Israel, the prophets were in charge of sacrifices along with the priests. Prophets were also called to be present on the battlefield for the sake of offering sacrifices before the battle, as was the case when Saul was going to fight the Philistines.

Samuel was appointed to offer the sacrifice, *not* King Saul. For indeed even the king had to submit to the prophet back then. But Saul became impatient while waiting for Samuel and decided to offer the sacrifice himself.

Then he waited seven days, according to the time set by Samuel. But Samuel did not come to Gilgal; and the people were scattered from him. So Saul said, "Bring a burnt offering and peace offerings here to me." And he offered the burnt offering. —1 Samuel 13:8–9

When the prophet Samuel appeared, he confronts Saul about the sacrifice that he offered out of place. And as a classic sign of rejection, Saul was defensive and said, "*I* saw the people scattering from *me*." Notice the words *I* and *me*. Saul was taking the men's fear *personally*. Instead of saying the men were fleeing the Philistines, which was the truth, he said *me*. This shows his faith in how many men were with him instead of faith in God who alone gives victory "by many or by few" (as his son Jonathon declared in 1 Samuel 14:6).

If Saul would have immediately repented to Samuel for offering the sacrifice, I believe things would have been much different.

Rejection's Filter

Saul took their fear of the Philistines personally. Rejection always takes things personally, becoming defensive, and thus never allows us to see or hear things properly. Remember, the most commons signs of rejection are being defensive and taking things personally.

I call it the "filter" of rejection because the spirit speaks and deceives you in what you hear and will not allow you to hear the truth. Think about a filter

> The most commons signs of rejection are being defensive and taking things personally.

that cleans anything. You pour something in one side and something else comes out the other side. Most filters take out the bad stuff, but it can work both ways. Filters can keep out the good stuff if it's a demonic filter or spirit.

Look again at this situation. In 1 Samuel 13:5–7, we see that because of the number of men in the Philistine army, the Israelites "followed [Saul] *trembling.*" So they were already scared and it had nothing to do with Saul's leadership. As a previously successful battle commander, Saul should have known that it was not a personal issue that made the men "tremble," but rather the battle situation as verse 6 says, "When the men of Israel saw that they were in a strait (for the people were hard pressed) then the people hid themselves."

But Saul's root (filter) of rejection caused him to misunderstand the situation. He looked to the people, not to God. Their reaction was more important than God's confirmation to him as king! Because Saul took their actions personally, we see a sure sign of rejection. Remember, they were already fearful, they were already fleeing, but rejection caused Saul to take their leaving personally, and it says he "forced himself" (13:12). Don't miss that point. When you are under rejection, you will force situations, relationships, decisions, and more.

Rejection causes a lack of trust in God's provision, trusting the "arm of the flesh" (see Jeremiah 17:5) and taking matters into our own hands instead. We experience many failures because we rush into situations because we can't wait for God to work in our lives.

Saul tried to bring success too soon by offering the sacrifice too soon, forfeiting the blessing of the prophet and God Himself, which was for success in battle. The reason rejection has a hard time letting us wait on the Lord is because it says to our hearts, "God does not care about you. He is not here for you. You are on your own and you better make it happen by yourself." Remember, demons train us by speaking to us, thus creating mindsets, behaviors, and finally our character.

Many people in the marketplace get into trouble this same way. As soon as an insecure person is promoted, they begin to be controlling or force situations, becoming a leader that people don't want to be around because they are not secure in their hearts. This is exactly what happened to Saul.

Slaves Who Become Kings

Let's look at Proverbs 30:21–22 to shed more light on this situation.

> Under three things the earth quakes, and four it cannot bear up: Under a slave when he becomes king,...under an unloved woman when she gets a husband.

What does this passage of scripture mean? It means that when someone gets power and authority, or other external affirmations, yet doesn't have the security to handle it, they become abusive, defensive, and controlling because, as the proverb says, they are still a slave. Have you ever been around an insecure leader? They can't take much advice because it feels like criticism to them. They can't lead because they want to please the plethora of opinions around them and thus never have clear direction. They can't handle conflict because they see it as a personal challenge instead of a corporate one.

The woman in the above proverb is similar to the slave. Both have a view in their own hearts of being less than others around them, being unloved, unworthy, and unfit. So when promotion or love comes along, instead of receiving that love and promotion and taking on the newfound security and peace that it brings, they still struggle with those around them and always feel challenged, not sharpened.

Many women suffer from this in marriage. A husband who is secure and/or promoted will "awaken" the unloving spirit that the now married and loved women should have gotten rid of. When a woman is married, she should reassess her life and the rejection in it and receive the love of her husband. But if she is still a "slave" and unloved in her heart, there will be a constant battle in her home because she can't receive love. She is thus still competing with those in her house and with herself. It's not a pretty situation.

The unloved woman and the slave-leader are dangerous to those around them. Don't be one. Receive love today and work to continue receiving God's affirmation of you. Saul should and could have done this. God confirmed him publicly twice to help drive out the rejection, but Saul didn't assimilate his promotion and he continued to look to man for approval and not receive God's approval. The deeper truth is this: Saul was still searching for his father's approval.

The desire for approval from his men was so strong that it led to rebellion, and this desire was fed by the voice of rejection inside him. Saul took on the role only the prophets were given, that of offering the sacrifice. This was his first rebellion that the spirit of rejection led him into, but not the last. His insecurity caused him to force himself to do things beyond his realm of authority.

The Blame Game

Notice also that for his defense, Saul accused Samuel of being late, in essence forcing him to offer the sacrifice. He says, "Because I saw…that you did not come within the appointed days," (1 Samuel 13:11) as if he was innocent of his disobedience and it was Samuel's late arrival that caused Saul to sin!

> When we carry rejection around, we cannot admit failure or disobedience. All accounting of wrongdoing—or even honest mistakes—take on the nature of a personal attack to us.

When we carry rejection around, we cannot admit failure or disobedience. All accounting of wrongdoing—or even honest mistakes—take on the nature of a personal attack to us. Have you ever felt that way? That your "emotional boat" was listing, like a boat half-filled with the waters of rejection, failure, abuse, and sorrow? Anger had popped a hole in your hull and you couldn't take on much more water? That is how Saul must have felt. So when Samuel showed up and said, "What have you done?" in a pretty stern tone, it must have hit the root of rejection and caused the walls to shoot up!

When I first read this passage, I thought, "Well, hey, Saul was right. Samuel did not come according to his own rule of a seven-day waiting period." So I thought Saul was justified, you know, probably thinking that Samuel just wasn't coming at all. But in truth, God used Samuel to rebuke him because God knew that *Saul apparently didn't seek Him* for what to do and whether he should wait. So even though Samuel was indeed late, He rebuked Saul because we can guess that Saul did not seek the Lord for direction. He just acted impulsively. *Impulsiveness and lack of self-control is a another sure sign of an insecure person who has a root of rejection.*

> **Impulsiveness and lack of self-control is a another sure sign of an insecure person who has a root of rejection.**

Compare this with Saul's replacement, David. Each time the Philistines came up to battle the nation of Israel, David inquired and sought the Lord. Note in all these verses, when David was going to a conflict, he sought the Lord (1 Samuel 23:2, 4; 30:8; 2 Samuel 2:1; 5:19, 23; 1 Chronicles 14:10, 14). David waited on, inquired of, and sought the Lord before going into battle. His trust was in God, not man. Saul, on the other hand, was just the opposite.

If you are a Christian, no matter what rejection you have endured, you have a way out. Jesus Christ and His love and His voice can help. Saul was, and you and I today are, required to seek God when things aren't going well. But rejection says again and again, "You're on your own. Do whatever you want. God is not here for you!" But you say back, "Liar!" Rejection is a liar—you and I are not on our own!

Rejection already tells us day and night that we are a failure. To then have to admit sin or failure to another human, especially one from whom we want approval, is often too much for us. Saul couldn't accept his responsibility. Not accepting responsibility is often a *huge* signpost that we are under rejection.

After this sacrifice debacle, Saul was again given a chance by God to prove his obedience and fear of the Lord versus the fear of man. He was told to "utterly destroy all [Amalek] has." Saul disobeyed, but when Samuel confronted him about the sin, asking what the animals are doing alive, he did what most of those with a root of rejection do: *He again blamed others.* Saul said, "[*The people*] have brought them from the Amalekites" (1 Samuel 15:14–15).

Saul should have learned from the former situation with the sacrifice that something was driving him to do abnormal things (like lying to a prophet—bad idea!). He should have seen his behavior as "severe" or demonic. He should have seen that he needed some counsel from Samuel or a priest. But instead, he continued.

When Samuel pressed him further, Saul replied, "But *the people* took some of the spoil" (15:21). It's a big blame game for him. I can just hear Saul thinking he is not responsible, "It's not me! No, no, it's the people!" Not until Samuel's final confrontation in which he says that Saul has fallen into rebellion (15:17–19, 22–23) does Saul confess his sin (15:25). This rebellion eventually led Saul into massive control issues and witchcraft.

> If you often blame others or immediately point out others' shortcomings when they point out something you did wrong, you have a root of rejection in your life.

If you have a hard time accepting correction, criticism, and advice of any kind, you have a root of rejection in your life. If you often blame others or immediately point out others' shortcomings when they point out something you did wrong, you have a root of rejection in your life. You will never have healthy relationships if you don't destroy this rejection. You will always beat yourself up and blame others. You will not grow because people's counsel won't be received because it's not counsel; in your mind it's an attack. Saul exhibits this perfectly. When Samuel confronted him, he said the people did it!

Saul and the Fear of Man

I define the fear of man as I would the fear of the Lord. To fear the Lord is to respect, revere, and worship Him, to value His opinion of us. To fear man is to give too much respect, reverence, and, yes, even worship to his or her opinion of us. God calls this idolatry. Proverbs 29:25 says,

> The fear of man proves to be a snare, but those who *trust* in the Lord will be exalted.

Trusting in God gives exaltation, but fear of man must then bring the opposite—demotion!

Do you see Saul's lack of trust in the Lord by offering a sacrifice too soon, by blaming the people, and by not obeying Samuel's commands? Instead of being exalted as king, he has the kingdom taken from him (15:26, 28). Exactly as the proverb says, trusting in God gives exaltation, but fear of man must then bring the opposite—demotion!

Important for us to note is that Saul, in a moment of honesty, reveals the fruit of his root of rejection. When explaining to Samuel why he did not obey his orders, Saul says:

> "Because I feared the people and listened to their voice."
>
> —1 Samuel 15:24

Yes, Saul had a spirit of rejection that led him to fall into the snare of the fear of man. The NIV Bible translates Proverbs 29:25, "The fear of

man brings a snare, but those who trust in the Lord will *escape trouble.*"
Boy, Saul sure didn't escape any trouble; he just kept getting into it!

When reading these passages, remember that the fear of man means
desiring human approval more than the approval of God. It means we
want to listen to our peers, family, friends, or others *too much.* It means
to reverence their voice or to *idolize* their opinion. This is the opposite
of the reverence or the fear of God. While we all should listen to wise
counsel, His voice is all that matters. We must align with Him only. That
is why throughout the Old Testament we are warned by the Lord to
"listen to *[His] voice*" (Exodus 15:26; 19:5; Deuteronomy 30:20).

Even after all that the Lord had done for him, Saul wanted the
approval of the masses. Rejection always wants and even craves the approval of man. It's what leads most of us into sin—we want to be cool,
hip, accepted with the "in" crowd, loved by the ladies, chased by the men, etc. Today, it's called political correctness.

> Saul should have dealt with his rejection by acknowledging God's love for him in choosing him, just as we should resist it today by acknowledging God's choice of us.

Saul wanted to be popular with
those around him—like some politicians
I know! "Is that so bad?" you ask. When
it leads to rebellion, it is! Saul ultimately
did not trust in the Lord's love, calling,
and destiny for him. This will always
lead to sin, I guarantee it. It caused Saul
to attempt the murder of David and to hunt him like a dog for years (1
Samuel 18:10–11; 24:14). Perhaps Saul had a bad childhood or school
days or a bad marriage. We know that some despised him (1 Samuel
10:27). But why would that matter so much when we see God blessing
him? We know that God showed great approval for Saul in the natural
realm. His behavior points to something supernatural as the source of
his actions. It's like a rich man who steals, there is no natural reason. It's
*super*natural; it's spiritual.

It was said of Saul that "surely there is no one like him in all Israel" (1 Samuel 10:24). He must have been striking in appearance, but being good looking will not cure your rejection issues because rejection is a spiritual problem. Nevertheless, do not think that his being a victim of rejection pardoned Saul from his sin. Saul should have dealt with his rejection by acknowledging God's love for him in choosing him, just as we should resist it today by acknowledging God's choice of us. Saul's sin was *not* in having the past root of rejection, but in *allowing* it to fester and infect *his heart*, which led to rebellion (1 Samuel 15:23).

What rejection ultimately does is keep us from obedience to God and His word. When you don't believe God is truly for you and truly, actively working on your behalf, you will live a life of blame, defensiveness, rebellion, and lack of direction. You will never be a strong leader, spouse, parent, or child of God because you are still a slave in your heart and slaves have no identity, no future, no family, and no hope. Slaves will sin and rebel because, after all, what do they have to lose?

Only deliverance through Jesus will break you free from this pattern.

For Your Personal Journey

Key Concept:

Saul had opportunities to change the way he thought about himself, seeing himself the same way that God saw him—as a king. Failing to change his thinking and keeping his root of rejection meant failing at being king. The key that could have saved him was simply turning his heart to God to hear His voice and obey wholeheartedly.

Questions:

- Am I still a slave in my heart who is trying to become a king in God's kingdom?

- Has God called me something different than how I see myself?
- What does God want to say to me now that would set me free from rejection?

CHAPTER 7

PASSIVE REJECTION

I encourage you to read 1 Samuel 9 to get a sense of Saul's early life. The chapter begins with a detailed genealogy of Saul's father, Kish. Genealogies as long as this one in scripture often indicate someone of great importance and reveal their connection to God's plans for the one noted as their descendant. Saul has five generations listed in his genealogy, which makes it one of the longest in the whole Bible. It also says his father Kish was a "man of valor" (9:1). This is quite a title to have in that culture and indicated that he was a victorious warrior in the clans of the tribe of Benjamin, perhaps having fought and survived the infighting between Benjamin and Israel. This is the equivalent today of having a Super Bowl quarterback, Fortune 500 CEO, or a decorated veteran for a father. It was no small thing.

So here we have a famous, successful father who has a tall, good-looking son (9:2). What's not to like? This is the perfect king setup, no? But later in the chapter, there are some glimpses that all is not well in good ol' Israel. Saul's father had lost some donkeys and sent the number one son out to find them with what was probably his number one servant.

Note that it says, "Take *one of* the servants" (9:3). This is another sign of wealth in this family because Kish had numerous servants. The fact that he let his son pick one of them shows us that father Kish wasn't minding the store, or his son, very well. A father who was actively involved in his son's life would have made sure Saul and his servant were properly equipped for the journey. As we shall see, Saul was not up to the task that his father sent him on.

What is revealing is the fact that Saul, as the story unfolds, was pretty clueless about what to do in their predicament. In 1 Samuel 9:5, it's Saul who gave up on the search for the donkeys first and not the servant. Then in verse 6, it was the servant who knew there was a man of God in the village, and it's the servant who happened to bring money with him on the journey, not Saul.

Imagine this: Saul's father sends him off on a long journey and Saul is without any money. This shows that one, his father never fathered him enough to teach how to prepare for a journey, and two, that on the day he sent Saul off, the father didn't take enough interest in him to check on his provisions for the journey, including cash. Any good parent will definitely check a kid's money supply when going out for the night, not to mention a journey of unknown length and danger. There is here, to say the least, an absent father in Saul's life and the result is classic passive rejection. Saul never knew the care and concern of a father. He never had the sense that Dad would be there no matter what, and Saul definitely had no sense that he had what it takes to be a king.

Saul then is left with the void that passive rejection leaves—no identity, no sense of mission or purpose, no sense of his ability, and the worst part, no ability to relate to God as a father that would act on his behalf. Saul is afloat in life, like most fatherless children, left to fend for himself instead partnering with his God. I believe Saul wanted to do what was right, that he wanted to serve God and His people, but he was so inse-cure and so lost in his identity that he could not do so because of the root of rejection in his life.

Your father or mother may not have abused you, beat you, or done horrible things to you, but they may have neglected you, been invisible in your life, and acted like nothing more than housemates who met your physical needs, but neglected your spiritual and emotional needs. They didn't train you for life. This is passive rejection but rejection nonethe-less. It's powerful and it ruined Saul's life.

But here is the good news and the good part for us. We need not let it ruin ours! When you look at 1 Samuel 9:15–27, you see that God had great plans for Saul and was speaking to the prophet Samuel about him *before* Saul ever met him. God was working things out for him. Then, and this is very important to see, God did incredible things to *affirm* Saul, to encourage him, to let him know that *He*, the Almighty, was with him and for him! Since God is no respecter of persons (Acts10:34), He is doing the same for you, even right now!

> God did incredible things to *affirm* Saul, to encour-age him, to let him know that *He*, the Almighty, was with him and for him! He is doing the same for you, even right now!

The Attempt to Father Saul

Read 1 Samuel 10:1–16 and note the stunning details in Samuel's prophecy to Saul, telling where he would meet certain men and how many goats and loaves of bread they would have. The number three is significant in Saul's life. When looking for the donkeys, he passed through the valley of Shalishah, which means, "The three." Later as king, he got three chances to do what's right and redeem himself. He also had three attempts to kill David, but failed, and David had three opportunities to kill him, but did not. Three is the mark of the Divine. God was constantly showing Himself in Saul's life.

God fulfilled His promise to Saul that He gave through prophecy (9:9–13), showing him that He was actively involved in his life. Then He fell on him with His Spirit (10:10; 11:6) was literally changed, as Samuel prophesied, "into another man." God changed his heart (9:9) and gave him a willing spirit to follow Him and do what He had called him to do. God's blessing and anointing was so strong on Saul that the people even formed a proverb saying, "Is Saul also among the prophets?" So he was getting public recognition and attention and, yes, affirmation! But root of rejection was still very strong even after all that God did in signs and wonders and fulfilled prophecies for Saul.

Having someone prophesy over you and then having it come to pass is a miracle. Only God can do that and it is His way of affirming us and encouraging us that He is at work in our lives. It is Him saying, "I am here at work, moving things in line to bless and cause your life to come in line with My purposes." Saul had very clear words fulfilled and they were fulfilled rather quickly so there could be no doubt; but never underestimate the power of rejection and the lies it sows into your heart. But more than that, never underestimate the power of the love of God your Father and the truth that He can sow in your heart. Here is a wonderful promise about the power of love over rejection and the sins it leads to:

Love covers a multitude of sins. —Proverbs 10:12

On His Own?

I often wondered why Saul didn't reach out to Samuel or some other men of God around him for help. Why didn't he have a "Jonathan" in his life like David (1 Samuel 18–21)? One of the effects of fatherlessness is the belief that we are on our own and that no one really likes us. I know I felt that way most of my life. Rejection will always try to keep you from having close relationships. Saul was raised to believe, "Hey, if my dad can't love me, spend time with me, and be my friend, why would anyone else?" Now I know I am being subjective here, but I don't think I need to read too far between the lines to see it. He even tried to kill his own son, Jonathan, who became David's best friend and covenant brother (1 Samuel 20:33)!

Saul constantly saw people as pitted against him instead of bringing them into relationship with him. This again is a classic result of rejection. "They are all against me; no one is for me; I'm *on my own!*" Note 1 Samuel 22:8 where King Saul says, "For you *all* have conspired against me...no one of you is sorry for me."

King Saul believed he was on his own, alone, and isolated. He thought no one understood him or would help him. This is what rejection makes you think. "And since you are such a loser," as it says, "if you do ask for help, they will think much less of your sorry self and they will *further* reject you." This is the cycle that had Saul trapped.

> When you and I view ourselves, as Saul did, of being "less than," then we will live "less than" what God has for us.

When you and I view ourselves, as Saul did, of being "less than," then we will live "less than" what God has for us.

Rejection and False Humility

Look at what Saul said to Samuel after Samuel, the prophet of God, affirmed God's choice of him. 1 Samuel 9:20 says:

> "For whom is all the that is desirable in Israel? Is it not for you and your father's household?"

That is Hebrew idiom speak to say, "The very best of your nation is set aside for you...by God!" Wow! But in either a bad spot of false humility or just plain old rejection language, Saul replied:

"Am I not a Benjamite, of the smallest of the tribes of Israel, and my family of the least of all the families of the tribe of Benjamin? Why do you speak to me in this way?"

—1 Samuel 9:21

Now either this boy was just really young and clueless when it comes to addressing elders and men of God, or he was giving Samuel a back-handed insult and he was cocky. Either way, one doesn't say, "Why do you speak to me in this way?" I could be wrong, but the tone of this strikes me as almost narcissistic, sarcastic, and almost cynical. I am reminded of Mary's response when Gabriel appeared to her and said similarly amazing things. She said, "Be it done unto me according to your word" (Luke 1:38). Now that is how you respond to a word from the Lord!

In a further example of rejection and the fear and (false) humility it brings, when Samuel was going to publicly anoint Saul as king, we see him hiding. God had to actually give Samuel a word of knowledge (1 Corinthians 12:8) to find him (1 Samuel 10:20–24)! God told them, "Behold, he is hiding himself by the baggage" (10:22).

Hiding From More Rejection

Notice that the verse says "hiding *himself.*" Don't we all do that? It's our inner heart that we are so afraid people will see and reject. The rejected person is always hiding something, but mostly their inner thoughts, feelings, and fears. They think they're the only one and they see themselves as damaged and so they must hide.

Saul was afraid of failing as king. That much is clear. I can imagine his successful, overbearing father constantly pointing out what Saul did wrong in his life as a young man. Many, many dads who have succeeded in the world can't accept a son who is perceived in any way as less than they were or are. In a word, they over-parent. They expect so much from their sons because, God forbid, the son might embarrass the dad in some way. So many dads who are successful in life are really still very insecure. But for whatever reason, whether their own rejection made them driven for success or their parents drove them (Kish himself was very likely driven by his dad), important, popular, or successful dads often create very wounded and very insecure sons. I know because I've counseled many of them.

So we see why Saul is in such a state of unworthiness and fear that he can't even accept his calling, even when it was confirmed over and over again. Saul grew up unloved, emotionally unattached, unnoticed, and ultimately "un-fathered."

God did His best to father Saul by affirming him. God does that in all our lives by giving us mentors, friends, pastors, teachers, co-workers, and events that He wants to use to affirm us, as our father should have done. The question is, do we see it? Saul missed those fathering nuggets God had given him. In fact, I believe that Samuel was to have been Saul's spiritual father, but Saul couldn't receive it.

> God wants to affirm us as our father should have done. The question is, do we see it?

Rejection will not let you receive the good things God has planned for you. Rejection will not allow you to have deep, personal inter-relationships, especially with spiritual fathers and mothers because it says to you that they will reject you if they really knew you. As if God can't give you someone who will love you unconditionally! Rejection is a thief and a liar!

Rejection will not allow you to have a right perspective about the very people and relationships that you need for healing because for most of us, as in Saul's life, it trains us from our youth. Whenever a parent disciplines us, including God now as our Father (if you are a Christian), we take it that He is mad at us or withholding His love, instead of seeing His love in His discipline. Hebrews 12 makes it very clear that "God disciplines [fathers] the sons he *loves*."

Rejection is Almost Always Generational

The dynamics of generational sin and blessing are of great importance in the Bible. Leviticus 26 is a good primer. In verse 11 God says,

> "Moreover I will make my dwelling among you and *my soul will not reject you*."

Then He warns them what would happen if they reject Him. Then, after all the many warnings, He says, "But if they will confess their iniquity *and the iniquity of their forefathers*...then I will heal the land" (Leviticus 26:40,42; the land being a metaphor for our hearts and lives).

He then goes on to warn them again but finishes with this wonderful encouraging word: "Yet in spite of this [their sin], when they are in the *land of their enemies* [no less!] I will *not* reject them" (26:44). Wow!

So even when you and I are captive to the sins of the enemies of our soul—depression, fear, lust, pornography, adultery, anger, drugs, bitterness, unforgiveness, deception, etc.—*He will not reject us*! As my southern preacher friends would say, "Them's shoutin' words!"

Let's look at a few Bible heroes to see how this generational sin actually worked.

Good ol' father Abraham had a generational curse of the fear of man, which almost always leads to the sin of lying. Remember, fear of man is an *inordinate desire to have people's approval*. He lied to two kings, Pharaoh and Abimelech (both titles of kings), about Sarah being his sister instead of his wife (Genesis 12:10–20; 20:1–18). Then his son Isaac lied to another Abimelech. In fact, Isaac lied in the exact same way, saying that Rebecca was his sister and not his wife (Genesis 26:6–11). Then Abraham's third generation of descendants, Jacob, completely lied and deceived his father Isaac, saying that he was his brother Esau so he could steal the blessing of the firstborn. You can see how the deception got worse.

Look at you own family in this light. As a friend of mine says, go to a family reunion and take some notes; you'll probably see the generational sin!

I also see a generational sin of pride working in David and his dad Jesse, which led to lust. In 1 Samuel 18, the man of God, Samuel, comes to Jesse's house and asks him to line up all his sons. Jesse didn't do that. He just lines up the good-looking older ones. When Samuel says that none of these are God's choice, then Jesse brings in lil' David. His pride made him ashamed of David. Later in David's life, his pride causes him to lust after Bathsheba. He simply forces her to have sex with him, un-intentionally impregnating her. Then he arrogantly sends her husband Uriah to his death in battle and orders his commanders to cover up for it.

Then in the next generation, his son Absalom, when he plotted to supplant King David's throne, arrogantly takes his father's concubines and has sex with them in public, just to show he was brasher then his dad! So the lust in David's line, like the lying in Abraham's line, got much worse in the second generation. Then, as David murdered those in his way, so Absalom set out to hunt down and murder his *own father*. Can you imagine? Yet David did no wrong against his son. In the same way, David murdered Uriah, Bathsheba's husband, yet Uriah had done no wrong against David. He simply stood in the way of David's ability to cover up his lustful act.

I hope with these two examples you can see the ongoing principle of generational sin. Of course, God Himself warns us in Exodus 34:7 saying that He "keeps loving-kindness for thousands and who forgives iniquity, transgression and sin; yet will by no means leave the guilty un-punished, visiting the iniquity of the fathers on the children and on the grandchildren to the third and fourth generation."

I know I still see the spirit of rejection trying to work in my children. My wife, Susan, and I both came from piles of rejection and that spirit still tries to work in our generational line. So I know that when I discipline my children, they might hear the enemy say to them that we hate them and don't love them. If that goes unchecked and un-prayed over, it will get a foothold and they will believe the lie of the spirit of rejection. I can't tell you how many times Susan and I have prayed against the spirit of rejection in our family!

Absent Kish, Absent Saul

How did generational sin affect Saul? We see the soon-to-be king suffering from passive rejection and the identity crisis that shows up on the day of his inauguration. Saul's father never fathered him, then Saul never fathered Israel and the "children" he was in charge of. He did what his dad did—became a mighty warrior. Saul did lead the nation to many victories over the Philistines as his father did. But Saul was a king in the same manner in which his dad was a father—showy on the outside but empty on the inside.

The effect of Kish neglecting to father his son created a far worse monster than his mistakes. Saul become one of the most dangerous things on earth—*an insecure leader.* As Proverbs 30:27 says, he was "a slave who [became a] king."

> Therefore they inquired further of the Lord, "Has the man [Saul] come here yet?" So the Lord said, "Behold, he is hiding himself by the baggage." —1 Samuel 10:22, NASB

I think it is interesting that the New American Standard Bible uses the word "baggage" in this verse. I think that is so true in our lives. Saul's "baggage" was that he had an identity crisis—he could not see himself as king. In his heart, he was a slave to his father, not a son. You and I have baggage, which can be the excuses we make about our parents, our schooling, and our vocations that tell us that we *are not qualified to do what God asks*. We all have wounds, like Saul, but we all have access to an awesome Father—God! We all need healing, but we all can access God's amazing grace to step up to the role of being kings and priests in God's kingdom. The Bible says that we are a "royal priesthood" (1 Peter 2:9), and that we have been "made kings" (1 Corinthians 4:8, note the past tense of this verse).

> We all have wounds, like Saul, but we all have access to an awesome Father—God! We all need healing, but we all can access God's amazing grace.

Ask God to show you "Saul's baggage" in your life. Then ask God for the strength to embrace His *good* plan for your life. Even if your past is filled with pain, He doesn't mean for your future to be the same. We must not let our earthly generational sins limit what God has for us!

I can be pretty sure Saul's pre-kingly life wasn't so rosy. Sure he had money, but he lacked love and a relationship with his driven father. Saul thought so little of himself—even after he was "changed into a new man," even after prophesying among the prophets, even after seeing personal prophetic words come to pass in his life, even after the prophet of God told him he was to be king, even after God did miracles in his life—that he *hid* on his inauguration day! Now that is what an absent father and the resulting passive rejection will do to a person! Don't let that happen to you! This is why most Christians don't fulfill their destiny—they don't have the sense of their Father standing with them to lead them into greatness.

Passive Love—Passive Rejection

One of the marks of passive love (and thus passive rejection) is gifts. Many, many parents who are uncomfortable with personal intimacy will show their love, however sincerely, through gifts. Younger children might really like this, at first. But the human spirit was made for intimate interaction. While everyone has their own specific love language, I personally believe that quality time spent with children is vital in establishing this one main truth—*they have value.*

> ~
> **This is why most Christians don't fulfill their destiny—they don't have the sense of their Father standing with them to lead them into greatness.**

Dr. Gary Smalley's famous book, *The Five Love Languages* is an excellent resource you'll need to read to discover how you best like to be loved and how to best love those in your life. One of these love languages that humans speak is giving gifts, but gifts can also be a mask. The fruit of rejection is often the fear of people getting too close to us, so we stick out our hand filled with something nice and say, in essence, "Here, look, I love you." People see through this quickly, especially as children reach the toddler ages and they want more; they want—*you!* There is no substitute. So be aware of any wounds that are leading to the fear of intimacy and ask God to help you be vulnerable to those in your life.

The other manifestation of the passive love–passive rejection model is the *denial stage* or *hyper-spiritual stage* of many Christian lives. When we learn about the love of God and that we have a Father in heaven, we often stop working to heal relationships around us. We try so hard to "get it straight from God" and be spiritual, especially if our parents are deceased. But in so doing we often miss something very, very vital to our healing—the reality that God uses people to heal us. He does this for two reasons: one, it's closer to what we really needed but didn't get from those who wounded us when we were younger; and two, we all need to learn to "be Jesus in the flesh" to those around us.

Now don't get me wrong. I spend time every day communing in the spirit realm with my Father God in heaven, and it's wonderful. But

I also pursue men of God who can be a father to me and other brothers who can hug me and encourage me face to face. While I'm in this flesh, I need some "God in the flesh."

If you were ignored by your father and/or mother, then you need to pursue the tangible, physical love and affection of holy men or women of God in your life. It will bring healing to the indifference that you experienced at home. Susan and I actively pray for these types of relationships so we can experience what we missed as children and so we can be a source of real love to others. It's a powerful force in our lives. This is how you turn passive rejection to active love!

> If you were ignored by your father and/or mother, then you need to pursue the tangible, physical love and affection of holy men or women of God in your life.

FOR YOUR PERSONAL JOURNEY

Key Concept:

Passive rejection from a parent can be very devastating and lead to as much sin as if you had an abusive parent.

Questions:

- What situations of passive rejection can you find in your life that you might have overlooked because of the more obvious active rejection events?
- What signs do you see that may be showing that you are you following in the same generational footsteps of rejection of your family?

CHAPTER 8

THE SEVEN DEADLY FRUITS OF REJECTION

~

I n Dante's divine comedy, he lists the famous "Seven Deadly Sins," which have been written about and copied and promulgated for centuries. I admit I am also copying the Italian master's list with my own twist, but perhaps it will make you remember them enough to help you. I want to list for you the *effects* or *fruits* of rejection as it pertains to sin in our lives. I like to say that rejection and rebellion are evil twins. Rejection almost always leads to some form of rebellion, so I want to list for you the effects of rejection as it pertains to sin in our lives.

Your natural, ungodly, fallen human nature wants to rebel when rejected. If you are stamped with rejection, meaning your inner view of yourself is that of a rejected one, then sin will come naturally to you. Because sin degrades us, we don't feel so bad degrading ourselves with sin since we already feel degraded in our hearts. It's like a pig in the mud. He figures, "Hey, I am *just* an unclean pig, so I'll just wallow in the mud. It's what pigs do."

Of course, if you are in Christ, you are not unclean, but have been made clean by His cleansing blood. But many of us still live as if we are unclean and figure since I just yelled at my kids, or lied to my boss, or looked at pornography…since I *am* such a screw up, I might as well just go all the way and sin some more! We say this not realizing, of course, that our sins are all paid for—past, present and future—and Jesus has made us holy already. You are sanctified now (1 Corinthians 1:30), but you may not live that way because you wrongly believe you are damaged goods.

When I think of King Saul, I feel compassion for him and the wounds he must have had growing up, thus leading to the sins he committed and the pain and suffering he caused so many. I can also see he missed opportunities that he had for redemption.

Here's the list of the bad fruit of rejection. While you read, be sure to look up the verses and see how it might apply to your own life. We learn so much from our own mistakes, but wouldn't you rather learn from other people's mistakes without needing to make your own? It's a lot less painful!

Selfishness

Samuel himself twice told Saul his rightful reign was over (1 Samuel 13:14; 15:28). Even after David was anointed king (1 Samuel 16:13), Saul refused to give up the throne. There was no servant heart in Saul at all, but rather just a desire to feel good about himself. So he hung on to being king as long as possible. He never really served others, because in order to serve, you have to be secure and Saul was very insecure!

Perhaps you can relate. Perhaps it is hard for you to say, "I am sorry," or admit wrong. Do you have to have the last word or control situations? Rejection is lurking in your heart and it leads to selfishness. When you are secure, you can promote others. Saul should have stepped aside and submitted to David and his anointing. He did not. It was all about him. It was all about his title and his position. He thought all he had in life was being king, so even after Saul admitted that David was going to be king and was more righteous, he asked selfishly to have David swear to bless his family (1 Samuel 24:20–21). Saul should have said, "My king, I am at your mercy; do what you deem right." Saul was selfish to the end. He couldn't even see the goodness in the heart of David, who spared his life three times!

A story from chapter 14 reveals the height of Saul's selfishness. He ordered everyone to fast until "I have avenged myself on all *my* enemies" (1 Samuel 14:24). He actually called a curse down on all who might disobey, which ended up including his own son Jonathan! He even ordered Jonathan's death (14:44)! This is the classic insecure leader I mentioned previously—the "slave who becomes king." Sadly, many leaders are in this situation, not having dealt with roots of rejection and looking to their position for affirmation, security, and comfort rather than their pure identity as a "son-king" anointed and appointed by God. And even worse, they don't see themselves as sons, but rather workers for God.

If you are a leader, even of your own home or business, much less the house of God, ask yourself these difficult questions:

- Are others suffering because you want to have your way?
- Do others at your workplace, church, or family pay a price for your selfishness? Rejection in your heart will cause this everywhere you go.
- Can you truly step away from all titles, positions, and authority and be a "nobody"?
- Have you compromised to keep your position?

If you answered yes to any of these questions, ask God to show your rejection to you.

Control

Notice in 1 Samuel 18:2 where it says that Saul "took him [David] that day and did not allow him to return to his father's house." That was the beginning of control becoming a strong spiritual force in Saul's life.

In verse 11, Saul tried to pin David down, perhaps even kill him. Killing someone is the ultimate act of control! Did you know that you can kill people with your words? Scripture says, "Death and life are in the power of the tongue," and again, "He who speaks rashly is like the thrusts of a sword" (Proverbs 18:21, 12:18).

Then in 1 Samuel 22, Saul tried to control his staff members and those who worked for him or were part of his kingdom, even the priests. In the same chapter, Saul killed the priests whom he could not control (actually had someone else do the dirty deed). They wouldn't follow his orders of betrayal since they knew David was the real king (22:14) and when Saul perceived he couldn't control them, he killed them. How many of us have done that with our words or actions towards those we wanted to control in order to make ourselves feel better?

If a person accuses you of control, don't dismiss it, but rather ask the Lord about it and seek God to heal your heart. Then, if you are really brave, ask that person to go into detail to help you see the control in your life. *It's probably rooted in fear and specifically the fear of rejection.*

Another common method of control is through intimidation. Anger is usually the means of intimidation and that is what's next on our list. Are you using your anger to intimidate and get your way?

Anger

This is yet another result of rejection. We get angry because we believe that God has shortchanged us. We feel cheated in life because we feel rejected by those from whom we want approval. Others are advancing and getting where we think we should be, so anger and rage set in. We often hide it very, very well but it's there, seething beneath the surface. Sometime it surfaces in panic attacks, depression, or general anxiety (as many psychologists will tell you), or, of course, outbursts of anger at your children, coworkers, spouse, or family members. You *cannot* keep anger in forever; it will come out.

Saul's anger opened the door to a spirit of rage and only worship could calm him down or cause him to be refreshed (1 Samuel 18:8–10; also see 16:23). People with anger, rage, and violence often have at their root self–hatred, a sense of failure, and a great deal of unhappiness. They carry a deep sense of rejection, whether they know it or not. Saul did not like his life. He thought he was a bad king because the populace loved David (1 Samuel 18:5–8). This caused more rejection and more anger.

I can imagine him saying to God, "Look, I didn't ask to be king; You picked me, so why is this David guy such a thorn in my side?" I can imagine Saul felt cheated, short-changed, and generally sideswiped by God, even sucker-punched and caught off guard. After all, God made a big deal publicly about making Saul king, so he probably said, "Come on God, help me out; where are You in all this?" It does really seem that Saul was doing his best.

> Rejection in your heart and mind repels people. We are attracted to secure people and repulsed and repelled by insecure people.

But the people and the army and the priests could not rally around him. Do you know why? *It's because rejection repels people.* I will say that again. Rejection in your heart and mind repels people. We are attracted to secure people and repulsed and repelled by insecure people. Right?

I think I would have had those same thoughts. I would have said, and maybe Saul said something like, "If you wanted David to be king, why didn't you start with him?"

But God did want to bless Saul as king for a season and I believe he always wanted to have David as king eventually, but only after David was older and prepared. I believe one reason David got into trouble in his kingship (i.e. Bathsheba and Absalom) was because he was put into service before his time. Saul was to have been king longer, but again, his fears and rejection were the character flaws that made that impossible. So David stepped up after God could delay no longer.

Paranoia and Fear of Failure

Because Saul was now in bondage to rejection, he saw all things through a filter of suspicion, envy, and jealousy. He trusted no one. He was afraid of hurt *before it ever came.* We all have acted that way, no?

We put up walls and try desperately to avoid the appearance of failure. We fear failure and now we are striving in our life, ministry, or work even as Saul did (see 1 Samuel 18:29). We begin to scheme and plot against *perceived* enemies as Saul did with his daughter and David (18:21).

Notice again how Saul declared that all his staff members are against him when he said, "*All of you* have conspired against me" (1 Samuel 22:8). This is paranoia; pure and simple Saul no longer trusted God and His good word spoken over him. Fearing perceived rejection makes (perceived) enemies, and though none of it is real, eventually it will become real. This paranoia will cause you to attack or reject before being rejected. It will put you on the defensive before there is actually anything to defend against! Before anyone actually attacks you, you will attack him or her, just to be sure you don't get hurt. This is the work of a root of rejection.

> This paranoia will cause you to attack or reject before being rejected. It will put you on the defensive before there is actually anything to defend against!

Saul "thought of himself" as rejected so he projected that rejection on those around him. Of course the Bible already states this truth when it says "as a man thinks in his heart, so he is" (Proverbs 23:7 NASB).

The final stages of rejection are not just experiencing the rejection, but also the fear of it. This is when we can no longer deliver ourselves and are in bondage to the spirit.

Jealousy

After David's victory, Saul became suspicious and jealous of him (1 Samuel 18:8, 9). Since rejection makes us insecure, we now look to material things or success to cover the wound. We compare ourselves to others and let a spirit of competition into our hearts. Saul said, "They have ascribed to David ten thousands but to me they have thousands. What more can he have but the kingdom?"

The "they" here in this verse are the people, so Saul next saw the people as against him, ascribing more success to David than himself and, of course, this breeds more suspicion. When jealousy thrives, friends are turned to enemies. People who have roots of rejection often have a hard time having close friends because they fear the closeness will bring rejection. They are constantly suspicious of motives. Note again where it says, "Saul looked at David with *suspicion* from that day on" (1 Samuel 18:9). He feared David, though he once called him a son.

> When jealousy thrives, friends are turned to enemies. People who have roots of rejection often have a hard time having close friends.

Reading 1 Samuel and studying Saul's life, you clearly get the impression that he was a loner with no close friends. That is the work of rejection. Suspicion, jealousy, and paranoia make for bad friendships and will eventually kill them or keep them at a distance at best. Many supposedly successful pastors I know have confessed to me that they have no close friends. Every one of them had a spirit of rejection.

Notice how in the midst of Saul's rejected life, we see a picture of the absolute opposite—Jonathan, Saul's son, becoming very, very close friends with David. God is trying to show us something here in the picture of two kings who are both called by God—one very unsuccessful because of rejection and the other very blessed because he was secure in God.

Self-Pity

Notice what Saul said in 1 Samuel 22:8, "Is there none of you who is *sorry for me?*" Most of us would have been like Saul at this point and felt like a victim, and this reveals another attack of rejection, which is the demon spirit of self-pity. Demons do work in groups, as any wise enemy would. Why work alone when working with others can bring more control over your enemy?

So self-pity comes in with the spirit of rejection very quickly if we don't stop it in its tracks. It whispers in your mind so that you think its voice is your own thought, "*Everyone* hates me. Poor me. Why is *everyone* against me? I don't have *any* real friends. I'll *never* be happy or loved." In this case rejection would still be the "strongman" that Jesus taught us about in Mark 3:27 and he is "charge" of self-pity as well as many other demons (see also Matthew 12:42-44).

You will notice I emphasized what I call "the extreme words of the demonic." One mark of demons is that they always use extreme words and paint extreme pictures in your mind. If you have rejection in your life, you know what I am talking about and will have used some of these same phrases: always, never, everyone, any, forever, etc., etc.

While self-pity is very similar to rejection, it is a separate demon that has its own operation and must be cast out. It says that we are a victim of someone else's sin. In other words, "It's not my fault." While initially this may be true, now you can choose to believe what God says about you, just as Saul should have. He was king after all, so why be insecure? He had access to the Word of God, the priests of the Lord, and to a powerful prophet of God. But he was listening to the voice of rejection, self-pity, fear, and jealousy and not the voice of God spoken through His prophet Samuel.

When we are in bondage to a spiritual force, whether we are a king or not, we need the power of God to set us free. Saul, like many of us, used pride to cover his rejections, and that pride also kept him from humbling himself before God to get the ministry he needed.

Other marks of self-pity are feeling sorry for yourself, lethargy, apathy, listlessness, and lack of drive or desire. You will especially notice how self-pity acts like a drug. When we meditate on it, self-pity anesthetizes us. It is like a depressant. It can become like a little thing that we pet when we feel sad and sorry for ourselves. Let me say this again: *This thought pattern is from hell and it is demonic.* It must be cast out in Jesus name! It must be resisted! You must not believe these lies that cause you to feel sorry for yourself! Look to the cross and behold the love of God for *you!*

> Self-pity acts like a drug. When we meditate on it, self-pity anesthetizes us. It is like a depressant.

Note that most times when people with serious rejection roots are being healed, they will rebel against the statement that rebellion, anger, selfishness, lust, and other symptoms are actually sin. They will often say that all this sin is a result of the rejection. They will often refuse to repent or even see *their own* sin of rebellion, anger, and selfishness. They take on a victim status—"My father never loved me, my coach hurt me, my mother hated me. I am a wounded person who just needs love." *Yes*, this is all true. But now you have *used rejection to excuse sin.* This must stop! This is now self-pity talking.

Rejection—the victim maker—tries to open a door, but *you*, the loved and valued person of God, must close it. Rejection was put on you and when you accepted it, the spirit of rejection came in your house (see Matthew 12:44). This is not a sin, *but continuing to agree with it will lead you to sin at some point.* You opened the rest of the doors and went from being the victim to being the villain. We are all both victim and villain, and we all can do something about it since we have access to Jesus.

〰

We are all both victim and villain, and we all can do something about it since we have access to Jesus.

Lust

Sexual lust, in my mind, is the most pervasive and addictive reaction to rejection. There is also the lust for power, as was the case for King Saul. The first sin I listed—selfishness—is similar to lust, but it is also different. You can be selfish without lusting but you cannot lust without being selfish.

It should come as no shock to you that sexual addicts are full of rejection. As we will see later, King David had suffered much rejection and he did manifest it in sexual lust, as did his sons. David's sin with Bathsheba is the glaring example of this, but his son, Solomon, was the second generational empowerment of lust. He really went off the deep end of lust having literally hundreds of wives and thousands of concubines, which were essentially private prostitutes (see 2 Samuel 16:22 and 1 Kings 11:3). King Saul did lust for power, position, and title, however, and that is a lasting and often most devastating manifestation of lust.

As mentioned in 1 Samuel 5, Saul's father was a wealthy man and I am sure Saul felt he needed to be the same. There is no question in my mind that Saul lusted for position, stature, power, and prestige because although he was told his kingdom had come to a close, he couldn't step down. David, on the other hand, resisted this type of lust and would not take the kingship even when he easily could have, but fell prey to sexual lust later in life. If we don't break the power of rejection in our lives, it will be very hard to be both *holy* and *humble*.

I strongly urge you to read the entire book of 1 Samuel about Saul's life to really understand how rejection works in our lives today. God put these men's lives on display for our learning and benefit!

FOR YOUR PERSONAL JOURNEY

Key Concept:

> Rejection causes us to sin in many different ways because we sense the wrong and injustice done to us and thus want to heal ourselves by getting into the sins that we think will make us feel better.

Questions:

- What sin can I see in my life that is tied to rejection?
- What am I doing today to break the rejection connection to this sin?

CHAPTER 9

W.D.D.D.
WHAT DID DAVID DO?

David—author of most of the Psalms, worshipper of God, famous king of the nation of Israel, and the Bible's greatest prophetic foreshadow of the Messiah—had several things in common with King Saul. Mainly, he had a not-so-great father and some not-so-hot brothers, and thus endured his share of rejection before he ever became king.

The Book of 1 Samuel chronicles one of most striking examples of two different ways people can react to rejection. In life you will see people experience rejection and fall apart, while others get rejected and not have it seemingly affect them. Why is that? It's because one had a spirit of rejection dwelling in their heart and the other did not. Both Saul and David experienced rejection, but they handled it very differently. Neither had particularly good fathers and I believe both had experienced a lot of passive rejection. David not only got it from his dad but from a bunch of his brothers, which, to a boy, is almost as bad as getting rejected by a father.

1 Samuel 16 records the anointing of David as king. Read verses 1–10 again and see how David's father Jesse had lined up all his sons in front of Samuel except David. Isn't it obvious that Jesse was somewhat ashamed of "little" David? Jesse could have, and should have, had a servant watch the sheep for a few hours while the man of God came to his house. When the man of God, the only prophet, comes to your house, it's a Hebrew tradition to show him your *whole* family, even daughters.

Now I want you to get the whole setting of how this monumental occasion went down and what it meant culturally. If you don't understand how it went down in the minds of the characters in the scriptures, you won't understand the level of rejection in David's life.

Scripture says David was the youngest and therefore probably the smallest. How often do we all judge by what we see and not by the Spirit?

Even Samuel was moved by physical appearances when looking at the sons of Jesse. Note what it says of Samuel's process in verse 6—Samuel thought Eliab looked good, but this did not move God to choose. Remember, Samuel was there on assignment to find the next king of Israel. Let's read:

> So it was, when they came, that [Samuel] looked at Eliab and said, "Surely the Lord's anointed is before Him." But the Lord said to Samuel, "**Do not look at his appearance or at the height of his stature**, because I have refused him. For the Lord does not see as man sees; for man looks at the outward appearance, but the Lord looks at the heart."
>
> —1 Samuel 16:6–7

Now, when all seven had passed by Samuel, he asked Jesse if there were any more sons. Jesses admits, sheepishly I am sure, that there was one left.

David and His First Big Rejection

Now picture this: David comes into the house with all the brothers standing before Samuel the prophet. The anointing oil is there giving fragrance to the whole room. The table is set for the sacrificial meal, the roasted lamb is hot and smells delicious, and then it hits him—everyone is looking at *him*! His dad has a sheepish look on his face (no pun intended for his shepherd son), and David's brothers are giving him "the look," being full of anger, jealousy, and the "you-better-not-get-anointed-little-brother" face.

David now realizes this was no ordinary drop-in by the prophet of God. This was a big deal and he was left out. Can you just imagine the shame and rejection he felt? The anger? We can see from later encounters that he must have already endured years of taunting and teasing from his older brothers, as is not uncommon amongst boys. Notice here also Jesse's sin and how it is passed down to his son: Jesse clearly had an issue with pride and the fear of man.

> The fear of man brings a snare but those who trust in the Lord will be exalted. —Proverbs 29:25

Instead of being exalted, we never hear of Jesse again after this incident. I think that is because God saw his heart and his rejection of his son David and was angry at the way David was treated by Jesse. I also believe that David saw his father's fear of man and lack of trust in God and that is why throughout Psalms, David wrote about his trust in the Lord (Psalm 34 comes to mind in particular). I believe David made a quality decision to not be like his father. Of course David also made the mistake of judging his father and that is *perhaps* one reason his son Absalom committed such treachery against him.

So David endured much rejection from his father, brothers, and many others when he became king, but I think the anointing session at his house left a mark of rejection from his father that never *totally* healed.

Yes, if there was ever an opportunity for rejection, this was it. And I believe, though I can't prove this, that David penned Psalm 27:10 from this occasion: "My father and my mother *have* forsaken me, but the Lord will take me up" (NASB, note the past tense of this verse).

Also notice that it lists "father and mother," in that order. I believe it's because that day, when Samuel showed up to anoint a new king, David knew essentially that his father had dismissed him. You can bet that all the other painful rejections from his father in the past came flooding in as well that day, and his mind was probably connecting the dots of the many times he had been rejected. But one thing we know for sure from our study of spiritual warfare, the demons were there to tell David how insignificant, little, and worthless he was. This is how the spirit of rejection works. He takes situations like this and speaks endlessly to his victim about how unloved and unwanted he is. Then the rejected one has to decide whether or not to accept the lies he hears in his spirit. Let's look at some opportunities David had for rejection and how he handled them.

> Demons were there to tell David how insignificant, little, and worthless he was. The rejected one has to decide whether or not to accept the lies he hears in his spirit.

"Oh Brother Where Art Thou?"

If you have ever had siblings, you know how jealousy can cause rejection. Look at how David's brothers treated him after he became the anointed one. David was told by his father to take some food down to his brothers who were in the battle camp against the Philistine army, which he does (1 Samuel 17). Remember that being a man in this culture meant fighting as a warrior; those who took care of hearth and home were women and children.

So the fact that David was either too young or for some other reason not able to go to war is already, in his mind, a strike against him. Because he later on became an awesome and feared warrior, we know he was able to fight, but I can only assume that he wasn't fighting with his brothers because he was too young to fight in the mind of his father and the culture. This would put David somewhere between ten to twelve years old. So when you read about him killing Goliath, get a picture of a very young boy, not even a young man.

When David arrived at the battle lines and heard the daily taunting of the army of Israel, he simply asked (in our vernacular), "What's up with this Goliath guy?"

But look at his brothers' reaction. They hear David's inquiry and get very mad:

> Now Eliab his oldest brother heard when he spoke to the men; and **Eliab's anger burned against David**, and he said, "Why did you come down here? And with whom have you left those **few** sheep in the wilderness? I know your pride and the insolence of your heart, for you have come down to see the battle." And David said, "What have I done **now**? Was it not just a question?"

What's a kid brother to do? He can't even ask about a little war news without getting in trouble. I believe David responded again by crying out to God with his broken and rejected heart. His father dismissed him, and now even his whole family seems to have rejected him. In his pain, he does what we all need to do—he cried out to God. Here are a couple of examples:

> A father to the fatherless…is God in His holy habitation.
> —Psalm 68:5

> Even my own brothers pretend they don't know me; they treat me like a stranger. —Psalm 69:8

I believe David's brothers are referenced here as he poured out his heart to God in prayer and song. His brothers sure didn't want their little brother to get ahead of them. Perhaps they thought David should have taken a lesson from Joseph and *his* nasty brothers! But God allows promotion to be public to test the hearts of both the one who is promoted *and* those around him or her.

> **David even felt that *God* had abandoned him, even though God never did abandon David.**

David knew rejection. From his mentor, King Saul, hunting him like a dog, to his dad being ashamed of him, to his own brothers hating him, he felt alone, unwanted, unloved, and very much rejected. Indeed, he was a type of the Christ to come.

That is why he penned Psalm 22:1 and Jesus quoted it, "My God, My God why have you forsaken me?"

I can imagine that at times, David even felt that *God* had abandoned him, even though God never did abandon David.

David's Key

So what did David do that was different? How did he survive all that rejection? Perhaps Psalm 73 is the answer. Note how the Psalmist was tormented by the unfairness of how the righteous and wicked seemed to end up in the same place in life, or at least so it seemed for a moment.

But as for me, my feet had almost stumbled; my steps had nearly slipped. **For I was envious of the boastful, they are not in trouble as other men, nor are they plagued like other men...***Surely I have cleansed my heart in vain*...when I thought how to understand this, it was too painful for me— **until** I went into the sanctuary of God; **then I understood their end**. —Psalm 73:2–3, 13, 16

Do you see it? The Psalmist thought living a godly life was of no reward. Could David have felt this way? Of course. Although this psalm is attributed to Asaph, who studied under and was mentored by David, I believe it sums up David's trials. All those who hurt David—the arrogant brothers, the wicked King Saul, and all the others—seemed to be just fine. *But then he came before God in the sanctuary and got an eternal perspective.*

> The difference between the two kings was that David sought God; Saul did not.

You, too, can access your proper perspective on life's hurts and rejection by entering the sanctuary of God. *This* was the difference between the two kings, Saul and David. *David sought God; Saul did not.* We never see any verses that show Saul seeking the Lord, praying to the Lord, or worshipping the Lord. We know he did offer a sacrifice, but there is little to no intimacy there; it was a legal transaction to secure God's blessings for battle. David on the other hand wrote, "Sacrifice and offering you have not desired" (Psalm 40:6 and 51:16). David knew the legal side versus the personal side of offerings, which is why he penned, "The sacrifices of God are a broken spirit" (Psalm 5:17).

Saul was clearly focused on men and not on God. David was the opposite and it's what carried him through his many, many rejections. Without our eyes on God, we will become wounded, angry, bitter, sad, depressed—you name it! But God gives us a perspective in prayer and worship that lifted David, and can lift us out of despair and into victory. God alone can give this kind of perspective to help defeat the rejection we all feel. Note the verses that show David looking to God alone as his source of comfort:

> I will both lie down in peace, and sleep; **For You alone**, O Lord, make me dwell in safety. —Psalm 4:8

> **In You (alone), O Lord, I put my trust**; let me never be ashamed; deliver me in Your righteousness. Bow down Your ear to me, deliver me speedily; be my rock of refuge, a fortress of defense to save me. For You are my rock and my fortress; therefore, for Your name's sake, lead me and guide me. **Pull me out of the net which they have secretly laid for me.**
> —Psalm 31:1-6

Rejection unhealed and unchecked will cause you to strive and be premature in life. A secure soul will wait on God and not take matters in his own hands like Saul did with the battle sacrifice in 1 Samuel 14. David showed his *trust* in God by waiting until God took Saul out of the way before he would accept being king.

Going Vertical

Do you see how David sought God and had to trust only in Him? Just read the Psalms and see how he poured his heart out to God and how he complained of the many trials and rejections he suffered. I want you to understand that *David complained, groaned, and released his deepest emotions to God.* This is one of the main sources of healing—releasing your emotions to someone who totally understands—like God. Rejection wants to trap or hide

---

Release your emotions to someone who totally understands—like God. Rejection wants to trap or hide your emotions.

your emotions. What keeps a wound powerful is the hiding of it and the stuffing of the emotions that should have been released but weren't.

Most of this occurs in our childhood. We are rejected and hurt and want to say something, do something, or tell someone, but we either can't because our family system didn't allow that freedom or we didn't know how to express our pain. Many of the emotional issues you struggle with today are a result of wounds from when you were too young to even know how to express them on your own. They then become part of memories and memories don't really die. They fade, but the lie you believed about yourself, be it a week ago or twenty years ago, never fades. That lie became a habit and that habit became a lifestyle and that lifestyle became a destiny.

Now a godly parent will draw out of their children their feelings by inquiring of them when they see they are hurt so the child can release the emotion. But this is not the norm. When children get older, they can learn to rely on God and look to him as David did. We don't know how David learned to walk with God, but he did.

Remember that David could have taken the throne from Saul twice, but he said he would wait and let God do it (see 1 Samuel 24 and 26). Saul, on the other hand, tried again and again to kill David, even after David spared his life! Saul had then become a slave of rebellion, which came from a root of rejection. Saul was out of control as he pursued David time and time again. David, on the other hand, had control, and thus the ability to wait on the Lord's timing. David dealt with his root of rejection in the sanctuary of God. David acquired a higher perspective than Saul, as evidenced by these words:

> **David dealt with his root of rejection in the sanctuary of God.**

"May the Lord repay every man for his righteousness and his faithfulness; **for the Lord delivered you** into my hand today, but I would not stretch out my hand against the Lord's anointed. And indeed, as your life was valued much this day in my eyes, **so let my life be valued much in the eyes of the Lord, and let Him deliver me** out of all tribulation."

—1 Samuel 24:10-12

See how David really looked to the Lord to take care of him as shown by the words in bold? David knew that God gave him victory. On the other hand, Saul chose to try to kill the one whom *he* perceived was the source of his rejection—David. After all, Saul thought David was the threat to his personal success and happiness. Saul knew the people loved David and it threatened him enough to try to do something on his own about it. But David, on the other hand, wasn't about to get ahead of God. *One of the marks of a rejected heart is the fact that the rejected one can't wait on God.* He sees life as only up to him to make things happen. After all, in his mind, the rejected one is alone, on his own, without help from God and others. Since, in his mind, the rejected person is *defective,* he now must make things happen since God would never help such a one as he. Or so the thinking goes.

That is why the Psalms show us a rejected David finding healing in looking to God. David didn't get it all right, as history shows, but he does show us the way to healing.

FOR YOUR PERSONAL JOURNEY

Key Concept:

David was rejected, but because he had developed a "vertical" life with God beforehand, he did not go directly into rebellion like Saul did. He worshipped God and poured out his heart to Him. He complained, moaned, groaned, cried, and confessed his struggles to God continually, and God delivered him. David was transparent, not religious. Saul was too insecure to be transparent, so he become religious.

Questions:

- Are you imitating David's approach to rejection or Saul's?
- If you are more like Saul who looked to man to help him and not God, begin to spend time reading the Psalms and imitating David's model of pouring your heart out to God. In this way, begin letting Him heal you today.
- Ask God for greater transparency in your life.

CHAPTER 10

W.D.I.D.
WHAT DO I DO?

If you are like me, you have read many self-help books and may have noticed that they are great at identifying the problem, but not great at giving the solution. I hope to change that. I have spent much time getting healed from the sexual abuse of my childhood and the rejection of my family and people in the Church.

I have read many books and walked with the Lord for many years, allowing Him to do all I know to heal a broken heart. While I am not done, God has done miracles of healing of my life. I am much farther along today because of His grace, mercy, and wisdom. I hope you will be helped by the solutions I will suggest.

It is important to note that this book is the *first* of *two*. My second book, *Rejection Healed,* and the workbook that goes with it go into more detail on how to be healed and made whole in your heart.

The Power of Perspective

In one of my favorite movies, *Ratatouille*, there is a line by the great food critic, Ego, when he goes to review the restaurant, Gusto's, where a rat has helped a young boy become a famous chef. When the waiter comes out trembling before the food critic, who has the power to shut down any restaurant with a bad review (this is very true; I know, I used to own a restaurant), he asks the critic what he would like.

The critic replies, "A little perspective. That's it. I'd like some fresh, clear, well-seasoned perspective."

The waiter is understandably confused at this request, prompting the critic to snap, "Very well. Since you're all out of perspective...I'll make you a deal. You provide the food, I'll provide the perspective."

The rat-chef decides to serve a humble peasant dish, ratatouille, and the critic is so amazed that he ends up being the one who gets "perspective."

Perspective can indeed be a powerful tool in our lives. It normally comes from one who has "been there, done that"—the expert, the one who's been to the mountain top and seen things in a whole new light. Our teachers are to provide us with perspective. God, being the ultimate teacher, has the ultimate perspective.

A great example of perspective comes from Numbers 13–14 when Moses sent out scouts to spy out the land into which they were to go. Twelve men went out and came back and ten of them declared a bad report. While they brought back clusters of grapes so big that they had to be carried on a pole and confessed, "Surely the land does flow with milk and honey" (13:27), they also said, "We are *not* able to go up against this people for they are too strong for us" (13:31). While they said the land was good, their perspective on the task before them was wrong. They focused on the size of the people in the land, not on the size of their God.

Now remember, these are the people who had seen the ten plagues poured out on an entire nation, the Red Sea part, were fed supernaturally from heaven, and watched God lead them with a cloud by day and a pillar of fire by night. No wonder God said, "How long will this people spurn Me? And how long will they not believe in Me, despite all the signs which I have performed in their midst?" (Numbers 14:11).

One of the most powerful workings of rejection is that it warps, twists, and darkens our perspective—we just don't see God. We focus on our abusers, our problems, our struggles and pains, all of which is quite normal, but only at first. But as we draw near to God, one of the key things He wants to do is cause us to see Him—His glory, power, heart of compassion, and most of all, His love for us. Is it any wonder that Jesus starts off His ministry by healing and delivering people and telling us that the Father cares for us more than the sparrows He feeds every day? The Word of God is meant to give us *perspective—the correct lenses through which to see our pain. Perspective is how you see, and how you see is everything, for if you do not see or see poorly, you will surely stumble over and over again.*

So let's not be like the spies who always saw the bigness of the problem facing them, but instead be like Caleb and Joshua who said, "If the Lord is pleased with us, He will bring us into the land and give it to us; a land flowing with milk and honey" (Numbers 14:8).

Now let's get some perspective on rejection. Imagine what it would be like in a war, under fire, down in a foxhole. There are bombshells going off around you, snipers are shooting at you, you can see and hear your buddies dying all around you, and the enemy is fast approaching your position.

All of a sudden, your buddy in the foxhole turns to you and says, "Hey, I wonder if the sergeant really likes me. I mean, he has been kind of cold to me lately. Look at where I am right now. Maybe I offended him last week; maybe I should see if I can shine his shoes for him sometime to get back on his good side." Can you imagine being in the foxhole listening to this? It seems completely crazy, but that is what rejection does to us. It totally warps our perspective, purposes, and priorities. Rejection twists perspective to make life all about us and healing our pain.

Step 1: Have an Outie, not an Innie

The reality is that the world is going to hell, billions are unsaved, drowning in drugs, porn, and other addictions, and if we have a spirit of rejection, you and I are focused on who likes us and who doesn't. We must see what rejection is doing in our lives and ask God to change our perspective. Don't let rejection make you inwardly focused; ask God to make you outwardly focused. Remember, the kingdom of God is the opposite of the world. Secular therapy makes it all about you, but God says, "Give and it shall be given to you" (Luke 6:38). That is how we are healed. Sometimes sick people need to pray for sick people in order to get healed! It changes their perspective.

> Don't let rejection make you inwardly focused; ask God to make you outwardly focused.

The truth is that *God Almighty* is *crazy in love* with *you*! Meditate, cogitate, talk about, sing, recite, and speak about this all day and your perspective *will* change. I know this can't make all pain in your life leave now, but it will help—a lot! My favorite prayer for situations or people that bother me is this: "Lord, let me see as *You* see." This is a powerful prayer that will change your perspective. Choosing to be an outwardly focused person is the first and biggest step to get healed from rejection.

The reason you must be outwardly focused is because it gets your eyes off your problems. The more you look at, focus on, and talk about your problems the bigger they become. This will cause God to be small in your eyes and the devil to be too big. That is what defeated the spies of Canaan and will defeat you! Ask yourself, "Am I an innie or an outie?" In other words, do you spend more time thinking about yourself or others?

Jesus' Perspective

The reason we have books and teachers is to learn from their experience, study, and wisdom. We can shorten our own learning process by listening to those who have perspective. When looking for someone who dealt with rejection and overcame it, clearly there can be no better example than Jesus of Nazareth. You don't even have to read the Bible to know that someone who is crucified has experienced severe rejection. From the beginning of Jesus' ministry, He was sought after by the leaders of His culture who wanted to kill Him.

> So all those in the synagogue, when they heard these things, were filled with wrath, and rose up and thrust Him out of the city; and they led Him to the brow of the hill on which their city was built, **that they might throw Him down over the cliff**. —Luke 4:28–29

> "But now you **seek to kill Me**, a Man who has told you the truth which I heard from God. Abraham did not do this."
>
> —John 8:40

He was accused of working with the devil (Luke 11:15) and having a demon Himself (Mark 3:22). He was mocked when trying to heal people (Mark 5:40). His family thought He was insane and tried to stop him (Mark 3:20–21). He was abandoned by many of His disciples early on (John 6:66), and at the cross, He had no place to rest (Luke 9:58). He was poor (2 Corinthians 8:9). He was beaten beyond recognition

(Isaiah 53:2–3),took on the sins of all the world (Isaiah 53:6), and finally forsaken and rejected by God the Father (Mark 15:34). That's what I call a pretty rough three and a half years of life!

We can assume He had a decent childhood and was loved by His family (Luke 2:21–41). We know He knew and walked with God as His Father (Luke 2:49) and that He was intimately aware of His mission (Luke 19:10; John 10:10). Ultimately, Jesus' mission was to reveal the true character of God's father-heart for us, showing us that the Father was to be enough for us.

So how did Jesus endure all this rejection and not let it lead Him to rebellion or any other sin? The answer is amazingly simple and yet not so easy to do.

Step 2: Do What Jesus Did

Jesus constantly meditated on the love His Father had for Him. Have you ever noticed how Jesus always talked about the Father? He talked about the Father because His Father was His life force. The famous verse, John 3:16, is about the Father giving Him as a gift to the world. Please read Matthew 11:25, 27; 18:19; 26:39; Luke 10:22; 22:29; John 3:35; 14:21–26 and notice the expressions like, "My Father." From verses like this, we can learn that:

- Jesus *knew whose* He was and what His destiny was (Matthew 11:27; John 5:36; 6:57; 10:30).

- Jesus *spoke His destiny* out loud. I believe He did this to teach us, but also to encourage Himself (remember that though He was God, He was also human).

- Jesus ultimately *trusted the scriptures* as a source of love and life and trusted Himself to them even when it came to death on a cross (Mark 10:33–34; John 10:18; 1 Peter 2:22–24).

If you will study the scriptures listed above, you will see the pattern of Jesus who had such a closeness to God that it allowed Him to be rejected yet not react in *any* negative way. This is your ultimate cure for rejection—the love of your Father in heaven. Whether it is a past hurt or future protection, you must do what Jesus did. Spend time with God in prayer and His Word and get to know His love for you. Meditate on it, read it, say it, pray

> This is your ultimate cure for rejection—the love of your Father in heaven.

it, sing it, tells others about, and write about it. Stuff the truth of God's unconditional love for you into your heart so there is no room for rejection to stay in there!

This takes *intentional* planning and effort. No one can do it for you. You must want to be healed more than you want to sit back and wait for God to do something. Most people I have met with severe rejection issues have developed some level of a passive mentality and therefore want to be rescued and helped from an outside source. They believe they are now helpless because of past experiences of being overpowered, manipulated, and intimidated, so they feel as though they can't do anything to help themselves. After all, they reason, "*I* didn't cause this pain, so *I* can't heal it." But this thinking is wrong. You are the one who can bring the healing process to you because you can seek the Lord, counselors, prayer warriors, and loving people around you to bring God's healing to you in real, tangible way.

Trust me when I say I relate to wanting to be taken care of. I remember many times in my journey when I would lie on my bed and cry—cry out for "mommy" to come and take care of me. I even began to want my wife to take my mother's place. Now part of this is the healing process of mourning the loss of a love you and I didn't receive, but eventually I realized that I needed more than just someone to pat my head and tell me everything was okay. I needed to get truth into my heart where the lies had been sown.

I'll make a statement that may be hard to grasp at first: The lie that was sown in your heart at the time(s) of rejection is more powerful than the lack of love you suffered from that rejection.

"How can this be?" you say. "My heart aches for that love that I didn't receive."

Yes, I know that is true, but the lie that came in at that time continues in your heart long after the rejection, and that lie has formed your *identity* for many years. While I will advocate that you do some of what I call "visual replacement therapy," which I discuss in my second book, I will even more advocate that you *expose* and *erase* the lie(s) that came during your time of rejection.

You Can Do This!

At this point, I want you to grasp that *you* are the biggest part of your healing. God is actively looking to help you, so if you simply call on Him to help you, *He* will give you the strength to do the work. David said in Psalm 22:15 that his strength was dried up. But then he says of God,

> But you oh Lord, do not be far from me, O My Strength, hasten to help me. —Psalm 22:19

The word *Strength* is capitalized in the text because David is giving God the name "Strength." So God is your strength *if* you call on Him to be so and *confess* Him to be so. That *faith* confession brings God into the equation. If you say, "Lord, you can't help me; I'm too far gone," it moves you into satan's realm and not God's. Now sometimes we do speak out negative things, and that is okay for a time, but we must not stay there and move from honest confession to self-pity.

While I would indeed argue that part of your healing will come from actually experiencing another human's love for you, I will balance that by saying that you and I must be proactive. If you don't have someone in your life who will genuinely love you yet, *you* must pray and ask God for them. Then *you* must begin to take the steps to develop a deeper relationship with *Him* who is the anti-rejection agent—God the Father. He is the antidote for the venom of rejection!

I want to help you develop Jesus' pattern in your life. Remember, He was physically threatened and then *physically* abused to the point of death. He was *verbally* threatened, demeaned, and castigated. He was *emotionally* wounded by the betrayal of His close friend Judas and the subsequent abandonment by His other closest friends. Finally, He was *spiritually* rejected by the one He loved the most—His heavenly Father.

Truly, no one has endured more rejection than Jesus. It was so thorough and so complete that now He can come to us and heal us no matter what we have experienced! That is good news. One of my favorite verses is Hebrews 4:15 (AMP), which says:

> For we do not have a High Priest who is unable to understand and sympathize and have a shared feeling with our weaknesses and infirmities and liability to the assaults of temptation, but One who has been tempted in every respect as we are, yet without sinning, let us then fearlessly and confidently and boldly draw near to the throne of grace that we may receive help in time of need.

Now if your mind works like mine, you might say, "Well, He was never sexually abused or raped or robbed or _____ (fill in the blank), so He doesn't know what I have been through."

I have thought about that at times when I have approached Him for healing. Then I remembered that He did see the event, and as one who has been human, He knows the pain of rejection and humiliation. He does know your shame, fear, and anger because, as God, He knows all things and see all things. Though Jesus has not personally, physically experienced all the different scenarios of rejection, He has experienced rejection in the deepest pains and He can heal you. Because no matter the specifics of our pain, the answer is still rooted in one thing—Love. That is why I remind everyone I can that the Bible is the *only* major religious book that states, "God is love." The Bible states that so we can know that it is the Word of God and it is the place to get the revelation of the One we need—God the Father—the lover of your soul and Healer of our wounds.

> No matter the specifics of our pain, the answer is still rooted in one thing—Love.

Let's summarize three areas for our lives that are keys to strengthen us and heal us: identity, words, and trust.

- Power of **Identity**. Jesus *KNEW who he was* and what his destiny was. Read Matthew 11:27; John 5: 36; 6:57, 10:30.

- Power of **Words**. Jesus *SPOKE his destiny* out loud. I believe he did this to teach us but also to encourage himself (remember he was still human). Read John 3:16.

- Power of **Trust**. Jesus ultimately *TRUSTED the scriptures* as a source of love and life and trusted himself to those verses even when it came to death on a cross. Read Mark 10:33, 34; John 10:18; 1 Peter 2:22-24.

The Power of Identity

Since the power of identity is the *most* powerful of these three and thus so important, I deal with it more in my second book, *Rejection Healed*. But I will say this much about it. Identity is not only who *you* think you are, but also whom you think God and others think you are. From this place you get your value and joy in life.

Proverbs 23:7 says it this way, "As a man thinketh in his heart so is he" (KJV). Who we think we are determines who we perceive we are in other people's eyes. If we get our identity, and thus worth, from what other people think, we will always be left feeling rejected to some level. The problem is through many acts and words of rejection as young people, we have a horribly warped sense of who we are. It is vital to know how rejection has shaped your identity.

The Bible gives us powerful clues how to reshape broken identities and how to avoid further identity issues in the future. I share awesome keys I have learned over the years on the Power of Identity in my second book on rejection, *Rejection Healed*. Be sure to read it.

The Power of Words

Did you know that words can curse or bless and have real, significant impact? I believe most people walking around on this little mud ball spinning in space are suffering from the effects of being cursed by other people's words and their own! We need to reverse the *word curse*. Study the story of Balak and Balaam in Numbers 22–23 to see more on the power of words to curse. Basically, Balak wanted the prophet Balaam to curse the nation of Israel because he knew the power of words. Note what happened:

> Then Balak said to Balaam, "What have you done to me? I took you to curse my enemies, but behold, you have actually blessed them!" —Numbers 23:11

Balak knew the power of words and was really mad at Balaam for not doing what he wanted! He didn't want those words of the man of God to help Israel; he wanted words that would help him defeat Israel. Because Balak saw how big Israel was and knew he could not defeat them militarily, he needed some other force to do it. He knew a curse would do it!

Whenever you see the word *oath* or *curse* in the Bible, you must understand it has to do with *words*. Words truly are powerful and I believe the second source of power to defeat rejection in Jesus' life, and in ours, is the words that can be spoken over us by others, ourselves, and of course by God Himself.

The Bible is absolutely full of verses to affirm to us the wonderful, life-changing power of words. Let me list some to encourage you in this truth:

- The world was formed by words: "By faith we understand the worlds were framed by the *word* of God" (Hebrews 11:3).

- Jesus' own title is the Word of God: "In the beginning was the Word and Word was with God and the Word was God" (John 1:1).

- Jesus' words were eternal life: "Then Jesus said to the twelve, 'Do you want to go away?' But Simon Peter answered Him, 'Lord, to whom shall we go? You have the words of eternal life" (John 6:67).

- Words can heal us physically: "For My words are life to those find them and health to all their flesh" (Proverbs 4:20-22; also see 12:18).

- Words will heal us emotionally: "Anxiety in the heart of a man causes depression, but a good word makes it glad" (Proverbs 12:25).

- Words bring us faith: "But what does it [the Old Testament] say? "The word is near you, in your mouth and in your heart," (that is, the word of faith which we preach)...So then faith comes by hearing, and hearing by the word of God" (Romans 10:8, 17). This "word" is literally the *rhema*, or spoken, word of God. It is the spoken word of God over us that brings faith.

- The word of God is spirit: "The words that I speak to you, they are Spirit and they are life" (John 6:63).

- Death and life can also be in our words: "Death and life are in the power of the tongue" (Proverbs 18:12). Our words work both ways and are truly powerful!

Jesus Needed Affirmation Too!

As I have said, the two main ways you and I experience rejection is from the words and actions (or inactions) of others. We would therefore do well to notice what *God the Father* did for His Son when He was about to embark on what would be the most difficult mission in history. Jesus was about to be rejected by God Himself, not to mention the three and a half years of conflict, rejection, and shunning by almost every human around Him that would come before His ultimate test.

Here is what Jesus' Abba Father did—He *spoke* over Jesus words of affirmation.

> When He had been baptized, Jesus came up immediately from the water; and behold the heavens were opened to Him, and He saw the Spirit of God descending on Him like a dove and alighting upon Him. And suddenly a voice came from heaven saying, "This is My beloved Son, in whom I am well pleased."—Matthew 3:16–18 NKJV

Now, you might think that a person who came down from heaven wouldn't need much affirmation since He had seen the glory of heaven. But remember, Paul said Jesus laid down all the rights and glory of His privileges in heaven (Philippians 2:5–9).

Jesus needed the same encouragement we all do. He was flesh and very human. Hebrews 5 says He "learned obedience through the things He suffered," and, "In the days of His flesh He offered up, with loud crying and tears, supplications to God," and again, "He was made like us in all respects and yet without sin" (Hebrews 5:8, 7; 4:15). So we know He must have been able to experience the same rejection that all humans experience. His father knew this, too, so we see God intentionally beginning by giving affirmation with words! And He even gave public words of affirmation, no less, when He said, "This is my son, in whom I am well pleased" (Luke 3:31).

So how about you? I know you have experienced, like me, some very painful words. Don't forget that the principle works both ways—blessing and cursing. Words can bless, heal, prosper, and encourage us, but if we don't get those biblical words hidden in our heart, we are still in a rejection-made love deficit.

So what do we do? We do what God our Father did for Jesus; we *speak*—to ourselves. We also need to listen to God and let Him encourage us. Jesus always said things like, "I do what the Father shows me," or, "I speak only what I hear the Father saying." Listening to God's words for us is vital! Study the gospel of John for best synopsis of this truth.

You and I need to speak over ourselves, out loud, words of life and destiny. What exactly do you say? Here are some ideas:

- *Who* you are (Galatians 4:6–7; Romans 8:15–17)
- *Whose* you are (1 John 3:1; 1 Corinthians 3:23)
- *What* God your Father has done for you (Ephesians 1:3–14)
- *What* your inheritance is today in the this life (Mark 10:29–30)
- *What* God has commissioned you to do (2 Corinthians 5:18)
- *Where* you are called to (1 Corinthians 10:13–16)
- *When* you are to do what He has called you to do (Hebrews 3:7)
- *Why* you have His love, power, authority, permission and commission (Titus 3:5–6)

In addition to this list, there are several pages of confessions in the last chapter of this book for you to use to activate this principle.

The Power of Trust

One of the most destructive residues of rejection is its ability to break our trust in God and man. When people reject, shun, shame, mock, and abuse you, why would you want to trust them again? Would you not avoid relationships with people who hurt you if you could? Of course. But sometimes we can't avoid people who hurt us, like parents and children. This avoidance really finds its root in something we can universally apply to everyone around us—mistrust.

If you remember that satan, who is behind all evil, does not want you to trust God, you might better frame the issue of trust. Satan wants you to think that any and all pain goes back to the fact that God did not care for you in your moment of need. Satan wants to get you to blame God. When we hurt, we naturally need to find the perpetrator, and since we all know in our hearts that God is ultimately in charge, we *assume* He is the one to blame. We rarely voice this to ourselves because we often know it's not politically correct, but still it lies deep in our hearts.

> Satan wants to get you to blame God. When we hurt, we *assume* He is the one to blame.

Now if satan can't get you to blame and mistrust God, he'll get you to blame and mistrust humans because he knows that God uses humans to love us, bless us, and be His vessels of encouragement. We must be aware of his schemes. Jesus again models the way to avoid this trap.

The Peter Principle

For you have been called for this purpose, since Christ also suffered for you, leaving you an example for you to follow in His steps, who committed no sin, nor was any deceit found in His mouth; while being reviled (and insulted) he did not revile (or insult) in return; while suffering He uttered no threats, **but kept *entrusting* Himself to Him who judges righteously.**"—1 Peter 2:21–23 NASB, AMP

This passage or scripture is really the greatest snapshot of a person who is free from rejection. I encourage you to read it several times. Go ahead, take a minute, we'll wait right here…

This verse is so very powerful, especially when read in conjunction with the history of Jesus' crucifixion, as recorded in Luke 22–23. What this history shows is the variety of rejections and abandonment that Jesus experienced. Then, as Peter points out, *Jesus did not in any way defend Himself!*

Who better to point this out than Peter? Remember Peter, the one who denied Jesus? He was the one who was so *mistrusting* of God and His protection for him that he called curses down on himself to show Jesus' accusers that he wasn't with Him (Matthew 26:72). Peter so wanted to protect himself that he disavowed all association with Jesus, yet he tagged along behind to see what is going to happen to Him! He was a torn man. Rejection does that, especially to Christians. *You fear the rejection of man, yet you want to be close to God!* You can't have it both ways.

Yes, Peter, of all people, knew what it was like to be so full of rejection and fear and insecurity that he denied the One who loved him the most, promoted him, treated him special, and took him into His inner circle. Yet he endangered himself by following Jesus to a place he knew would get him in trouble. How many of us live like this?

Peter was imminently qualified to observe how very much Jesus *trusted* His Father, but then contrasted it with his own life. Peter must have been painfully aware of his own mistrust while watching Jesus stand silent before His accusers. Peter suffered from the main infliction of rejection—the fear of man.

The fear of man proves to be a snare, but those who **trust** in the Lord will be kept safe. —Proverbs 29:25, NASB

The Danger of the Fear of Man

It was said of Jesus, "Teacher, we know that you speak and teach what is right and are *not influenced by what others think*. You sincerely teach the ways of God" (Luke 20:21). So here you see Jesus had no fear of man, or as the verse above says, He was not influenced by man. The antithesis of this is Peter. He was the one who had the first known revelation of who Jesus was. He declared, "You are the Christ (Messiah), the Son of the living God" (Matthew 16:16). But then later on when Jesus needed him most, Peter would deny his association with Jesus publicly because he didn't want to be rejected by those around the trial of Jesus. Peter's rejection was showing—and it almost broke him as it says he went out and "wept bitterly" (Luke 22:62).

The fear of man will not let you trust very easily, especially God. That is why people who have a root of rejection struggle with fear and anxiety. Because they don't believe God is there for them, they can't *trust* Him to keep them safe. Note that the scripture says that the opposite of the fear of man is to trust, and the fruit then is to be kept safe:

> One of the clearest signs of a rejected person is that they do well in groups, but very poorly on their own, alone. That is when fear sets in.

The fear of man proves to be a snare, but those who **trust** in the Lord will be **kept safe**. —Proverbs 29:25

Now if you know the scriptures, you might say, "Wait a minute, Peter was the only guy besides Jesus who walked on water; he was a man of faith and power!" Yes, Peter had faith. He had faith in the power of Jesus to do miracles—but only when Jesus was there. Peter was a different man when Jesus wasn't around. We can learn a lot about rejection from Peter. For example, one of the clearest signs of a rejected person is that they do well in groups, but very poorly on their own, alone. That is when fear sets in.

Separated from Love

Remember when Jesus and Peter first met? Luke 5 tells the story well. Peter and the boys go fishing and catch nothing. Jesus pulls up, tells Peter to try it again, and Peter argues at first. But when He follows Jesus' instructions, behold, the big fish miracle happens where Peter and the boys catch literally a boatload of fish. And what are the first words out of Peter's mouth?

> "Go **away** from me Lord, for I am a sinful man, oh Lord!"
>
> —Luke 5:8

Remember, rejection *separates*. It makes you think you are separated and alone. It makes you sin-conscious. Interestingly, Isaiah 59:1 says, "Your sins have made a *separation* between you and your God."

This is a fact, but the bigger and better fact is that God doesn't *want* You to be separate from Him!

What this passage reveals to us about Peter is that he had a deep sense of failure, fear, unworthiness, and general religious baggage about the love of God in his life. This is exactly like most Christians today that I know and how I functioned most of my Christian life. The words *Go away* are very revealing. This speaks of someone who cannot receive the blessings of God, someone who feels separate from God and who wants to stay that way, someone who lived rejected. That fish miracle brought the reality of God too close to Peter

> Rejection *separates*. This is a fact, but the bigger and better fact is that God doesn't *want* You to be separate from Him!

that day. It made him aware of his state. But Jesus wasn't there to condemn him, but to call him. Many of us are so used to living a "separate" spiritual life that we are actually afraid to get too close to God. When I teach my class on hearing God's voice, I find that even ardent Christians have trouble drawing close enough to God to intimately hear Him, at least on any regular basis.

A little over a year ago, the Lord spoke to me in my quiet time one of the greatest truths that He has ever spoken to me, a truth that I have meditated on many, many times and one that continues to speak to me and challenge me. He said, "The greatest thing love teaches you is how to receive." So when I look at Peter and his denial of Jesus, after all the love Jesus had shown him, I know Peter had a deep root of rejection. He could not receive the love and the blessings of God—not even some little, insignificant fish! Jesus tried to give him some perspective on this first "little blessing" by telling him, "Do not fear, from now on you will be catching men" (Luke 5:10).

This again confirms my suspicion about Peter because Jesus addressed his *fear*, and 1 John 4:17 states, "Perfect love casts out fear." So Peter, like so many of us, had not yet been perfected or matured in love. But his moment was coming. In John 20, after his denial, Jesus turned it all around for Peter.

So regarding the power of trust, let's learn from the Master. Jesus so trusted His Father's character and words (the Old Testament) that He put His life completely in His hands! But more than that, He endured such rejection and utter humiliation of spitting, mocking, beating, and more. Most of us would have cursed, reviled, spit, kicked, and then bawled and railed at God for allowing us to endure such pain and rejection.

That is why Peter's comments are so powerful, that "While being reviled, he did not revile in return" (1 Peter 2:23). Remember your worst day of rejection and imagine that even though you *could* have retaliated with all power and authority, you did *nothing*. Jesus affirms this restraint even more in the gospel of Matthew. While being arrested, He reminds His accusers that He could call down twelve legions of angels to help him, but of course He did not (Matthew 26:53).

One Verse?!

With all Jesus went through during His brutal passion, we have to ask the question, *How could Jesus contain Himself, remaining without sin, bitterness, anger, and revenge?* The answer is that He *trusted* His Father to justify Him—to vindicate Him and show the world His Son's innocence by raising Him from the dead. Jesus knew the prophecy about His death in Isaiah 53 and all the wonderful things it would accomplish for us. (By the way, if you have never read the prophecies in Isaiah 53 then please, read that chapter now!)

But concerning being *raised* from the dead, there was only one obscure verse in the *whole* Old Testament. Do you know it? Most Christians don't, yet Jesus said that He must be raised on the third day, "just as the scripture has said." But where is this verse?

Remember, as a human, He had to *trust* the Word of God just the same way you and I do. He had to *trust* and *obey* and let the Father perform what was spoken.

While being betrayed by His friend, Judas, He trusted the Father. While being abandoned by the twelve disciples, He had to trust the Father. While He was being whipped with a cat of nine tails and the flesh was literally ripped off His back, legs, and front, He trusted His Father. When the nails finally went into His hands, He had to trust His Father's promises. When He felt His life slowly slipping away, He had to trust His Father.

Even in His humanity, Jesus quoted Psalm 22:1, which says, "My God my God, why have you forsaken me?" So you know He felt the rejection that is beyond all other rejection. To be forsaken is the worst.

It means rejection without hope, no chance of recovery at all, left and abandoned forever.

Jesus felt that way because that is what God had to do with sin—your sin and my sin. God had to forsake, abandon, reject, destroy, and banish all sin for all time so all men could, *if they so choose*, be saved. Because Jesus became one with our sin, the Father had to forsake, abandon, reject, destroy, and banish His very own beloved Son. That is why scripture says, "He [Jesus] who know no sin *became sin* on our behalf, that we might become the righteousness of God" (2 Corinthians 5:21).

Jesus knew when He came that this is what would happen to Him. What could have given Him such a clear promise as to enable Him to trust so completely? Here's the obscure verse that Jesus trusted enough to die for:

> Come, and let us return to the Lord; for He has torn, but He will heal us; He has stricken, but He will bind us up. After two days He will revive us; **on the third day He will raise us up**, that we may live in His sight. —Hosea 6:1–3

Note that it doesn't even say, "On the third day He will raise *him* up, or "*you* up," but it says, "us." Who is us? It's Israel, or literally, all the children of God. But get this—the Messiah *is* Israel. They are indeed one, because they come from the same seed, the same Father, and eventually, when they become Christians, the same Spirit (that is why genealogy is so important in the Bible).

So, to God, whatever promises were made to or about Israel were made to the Messiah and whatever promises made about or to the Messiah also belonged to Israel. That is why Paul, under the inspiration of the Holy Spirit, wrote in 2 Corinthians 1:20, "For all the promises of God *in Him* are Yes, and *in Him* Amen, to the glory of God through us."

So Jesus saw this verse in Hosea and knew that it was for Israel, and for Him, and *all* who would believe in Him for all eternity. It was a promise to change history. But he had to *trust* the Father, and that is what you and I need to do when all seems lost and we feel the most rejected.

Step 3: You Are Not in This Alone!

Like Jesus, we also go to the Word of God to find the promise that covers our pain and brokenness and then ask God for the grace to trust His Word. Faith in a promise produces a new reality because God's word *is* reality (see Hebrews 11:1)!

But if you are like me, you might say, "Hey, I am too wounded and hurt to trust right now." The key for all those who have lost trust because of rejection is to *start small*. Jesus didn't start with trusting His death issue, but rather praying for the sick and various other miracles. He trusted God as a child through adulthood, with His ministry and finally, with His life.

> Jesus gave Peter the ability to trust by loving him and showing Peter that He trusted him. Do you know that God trusts you?

You, too, will have to start small, trusting in small issues, just like Jesus did. Peter had to learn the same lesson. He didn't start with miracles and church planting, but with eating fish with Jesus on the shore of a lake, being restored when Jesus was asking him if he loved Him, which must have been hard for Peter. *Jesus gave Peter the ability to trust by loving him and showing Peter that He trusted him. Do you know that God trusts you?*

Peter learned trust by failing Jesus miserably, but then being restored in love and trust. Jesus restored total trust in Peter by telling him three times, "feed my lambs" (John 20). I don't believe Jesus' words were a command, but rather a commissioning. And when someone is commissioned, they are entrusted with great authority. Jesus was in essence saying, "Peter I trust you, even after your denial of me, with the task of caring for my precious lambs."

Peter ended up being crucified, trusting his Father the same way Jesus did. I can only imagine that he performed as Jesus—no reviling, no threats uttered, just surrender. How was he able to do that? Because Peter knew how much he was loved and that his Father was going to make it right and take care of him. He knew this because Jesus Himself had trusted Peter with His most precious possession—*His children.*

Trust breeds trust. When you begin to trust your Father, He will trust you, and when you see more of His trust in you, you will in turn trust humans more and enjoy the acceptance of those around you. This is a great help towards healing from rejection. Do you know why you'll trust people more when you trust God more? Because even when people let you down, which they will, you will see beyond it into the heart of God and know that He is still there, loving and trusting and caring for you.

FOR YOUR PERSONAL JOURNEY

Key Concept:

We all have tools at our disposal to defeat the spirit of rejection. Jesus taught us through His example to use our words and God's words to strengthen our inner man. He learned His identity, value, and purpose, thus learning to trust His Father.

Questions:

- How has rejection damaged your perspective and your ability to trust the Bible, God, and man?
- Can you see a bit of Peter in yourself? If so, what can you learn from his life?

CHAPTER 11

YOU CAN DO THIS!

I hope by now you have recognized that rejection is at the root of much of the bad fruit in your life and that, while it can take many forms, rejection is ultimately driven by a demonic spirit. Satan himself, being full of rejection, is out to separate you from God and from others by lying to you about who you are and who God is. Satan and his spirits of rejection want to bring separation in your life. When you feel rejected, you feel excluded and on the outside looking in. Rejection wants to separate you from God and your fellow man because God is your source of healing and love and God often uses people to bring love into your life. I have endeavored to help identify the manifestation of the spirit of rejection working in our lives so you can see it and begin to deal with it.

I also want to offer some early solutions that will help you heal—words being the main one, and that is why I offer some confessions from scripture in the last chapter to get you started on a path to healing. Here are some parting thoughts to help best send you off into your healing.

Be Alert

Remember, rejection is sneaky. Really. Most people I meet don't readily identify rejection as an issue in their lives. That is why God had me write this book—to expose the spirit of it and help you identify it.

Jesus told us that we must bind the strongman so we can plunder his house. One thing I have learned about demons and how they operate is that *the strongman always hides*. He hides behind other more seemingly obvious or flagrant demons like alcoholism, lust, fear, anger, etc. But as I mentioned, the root to most issues is rejection. Imagine a life where you felt, every moment of every day, totally and completely loved by God, your spouse, your family, your children, and all your friends, from the time you were born! Imagine never having a moment of doubt about their unconditional love for you. That is a life without the spirit of rejection working in you. It's possible, but a whole lot of people need healing for it to come to pass. Yet this is exactly how God made man—to love and to be loved!

Receive God's Love and Love Others

After the Garden of Eden, God had to take the initiative. In comes His Messiah, Jesus of Nazareth. Never has so sinless a being loved such sinners as did Jesus. If you want to know and understand God, look at Jesus.

The Apostle John encapsulates this perfectly when he says:

> No one has seen God as any time; the only begotten God who is in the bosom of the Father, He has explained Him.
>
> —John 1:18

And again...

> In this is love, not that we loved God, but that He [first] loved us and sent His Son to be the propitiation for our

sins. Beloved, if God so loved us, we also ought to love one another. —1 John 4:10–11

That's it. God so powerfully, wonderfully, completely demonstrated His love for sinful man by giving us Jesus that it ought to inspire us to love one another. Jesus and His love in a person's heart *is the answer* to what ails our world. That is the essence of Christianity and God Himself—love personified.

You and I have all been and will be rejected, but it doesn't stop there. Love Himself is standing at your door right now, knocking, waiting to come into your heart in a new and fresh way. Lamentations 3:22–23 reminds us that God's mercies are *new* every morning. Let Jesus in right now. He made this promise to you—He said He came to "heal the brokenhearted" (Isaiah 61:1). He wants to heal your heart so much that He died to make it possible. Receive Him today. Close your eyes and see Him. Reach out with the eyes of your heart and invite the Healer to walk with you and talk with you, and then pour your heart out to Him.

David did that. Look at several key verses in Psalm 69 and then practice this in your own life:

David complained and was honest about his situation:

> Reproach [rejection] has broken my heart, and I am full of heaviness; I looked for someone to take pity, but there was none; and for comforters, but I found none. —verse 20

Then he chose to praise God:

> Let Your salvation, O God, set me up on high. I will praise the name of God with a song, and will magnify Him with thanksgiving. This also shall please the Lord better than an ox or bull, which has horns and hooves. The humble shall see this and be glad; and you who seek God, your hearts shall be revived. —verses 29–32

He then confessed who God is and what God thinks of him, speaking a positive word of truth:

> For the LORD hears the needy and **does not despise his own people who are prisoners**. —verse 33, NKJV

> The Lord listens to those in need and **does not look down on captives**. —verse 33, GNT

> For the ears of the Lord are open to the poor, **and he takes thought for his prisoners**. —verse 33, ESV

> The Lord listens to those in need and **does not forget his people in prison**. —verse 33, GW

Perhaps you have felt shame because you are a Christian who struggles. You think you should know better, be better, and do better. Yet in your heart, you know your own captivity. Be encouraged that, according to this verse, God, your real Father, does not despise you, look down on you, or forget you, but rather He takes thought of you and knows you are a prisoner and He promises to set you free!

Even as David declared, so can we declare: "The Lord is good to all, and His tender mercies are over all His works" (Psalm 145:9, NKJV).

You are His finest work and His *tender mercy* is over you today! Take it and enjoy it! Take *Him* and enjoy *Him*!

Seek out Help

Finally, earnestly seek out others to help you overcome the effects of rejection in your life. Trying to do it alone is part of why you are where you are today. Ask the Lord to connect you with counselors, pastors, and fellow saints, who can understand you and give you biblical prayer for deliverance.

You may contact our office for personal deliverance prayer. Our website offers names of ministries we feel are legitimate deliverance and inner healing people who can help you (763-300-7312, www.northfirenet.com). May His love fill your hearts and drive out all the works of the evil one! In Jesus, you are loved!

Before moving on to the final chapter of this book, which includes biblical confessions that will help you break free from rejection, please know there is much more that the Lord has shown me on this subject. There is a companion workbook that goes with this book, which includes the following:

- A summary of each chapter
- Study questions that review key concepts from the chapter
- Key scriptures to meditate on for personal growth
- Personalized prayer focused on the chapter topic
- Bonus questions for personal reflection and group discussion

I have also written a second book, *Rejection Healed.* This resource can help lead you to even greater healing from rejection and give you more tools for repairing the damage rejection has done in your life. I hope you will pick that up and its companion workbook by the same name. I know that these resources will bring healing in your life and the life of others.

FOR YOUR PERSONAL JOURNEY

Key Concept:

You and I have all been and will be rejected, but Jesus is waiting to come into your heart in a new and fresh way. He came that we would have life abundantly. Receive His life today.

Questions:

- Who have you talked to about the rejection you have experienced? Talk to someone you can trust today about what you have learned in this book.
- Seek out the help you need to receive the healing and freedom Christ came to give.

CHAPTER 12

CONFESSION AND FREEDOM

~

The principal behind this study and exercise is simple—God's power is in His *spoken* word. His power is the only power that can save or deliver us. His Word is inactive until we speak it and then act on it. It's like money in the bank that has never had a withdrawal made on it.

I am sure that before God said, "Let there be light," He had preconceived in His mind what He wanted the light to be. But it did not happen until He *said* it!

In Matthew 4, Jesus likewise defeated temptation by speaking the Word of God. In fact, if you think about it, He reiterated His own words from the Old Testament. He had enough confidence in those words, spoken thousands of years earlier, to defeat the devil during His incarnation! How much more should we trust them today!

Notice in Mark 11:23, Jesus says, "Whoever *says* to this mountain 'Be taken up and cast into the sea,' and does not doubt in his heart, but believes that what he *says* will happen, it will be granted to him." Jesus did not say we should think about or ponder over the mountain, but rather *speak* to our mountain.

Let us never forget that Jesus is called the Word. He is God in His ultimate will towards us:

> Who [Jesus] being the exact representation of [God's] nature, upholds all things by the **word of His power**. —Hebrews 1:3

> My son attend to my words, (consent and submit to my sayings) let them not depart from your sight, keep them in the midst of your heart, for they are life to those who find them, healing and health to all their whole flesh. —Proverbs 4:20–22, AMP

> Man does not live by bread alone, but by every word that proceeds **out of the mouth** of God. —Deuteronomy 8:3

So we see that God's written word has power that follows this pattern:

- Its dynamic power comes when we speak it and then act on it, but…
- We only act on it when we believe it.
- We only believe it when it becomes the dominant thought in our mind.
- It will only be the dominant thought in our mind when we meditate (read, speak, think on, ponder, cogitate, reflect, etc.) on His Word. We must hear it and hear it over and over again. Romans 10:17 says, "So then faith comes by hearing and hearing by the Word of God." (Greek "word" is literally *rhema*—the spoken word.)

- You will have to be your own preacher and give yourself a sermon to deliver yourself from whatever is coming against you.

We must start with confession and thanksgiving. Confession in the Bible is *not* primarily used to confess sin. Rather, the word for confess in the Greek means, "To say the same thing." We are to say the same thing that God says about our situation, whether it is sickness, fear, anxiety, sin struggles, or especially rejection.

The rest of this chapter contains biblical confessions focused on key themes that will help you reject rejection and be free from its hold on you. I've used the New American Standard Bible unless otherwise noted. I encourage the Amplified translation for meditation. For all of these verses, say them *out loud*. Remember, out loud. And let faith rise as you *hear* these words of truth come out of your own mouth.

Condemnation and Shame

Lord, I see that if I am bothered by the memory of past sin, it is not from You. Therefore, since You don't dwell on my past sin, neither will I! My sin was between You and me and it is no one's business. If the devil or anyone else tries to remind me of it, I won't let them.

I am living for You, so as Paul said in Philippians 3:13, I am "forgetting what lies behind and reaching forward to what lies ahead, I press on towards the goal for the prize of the upward call of God in Christ Jesus." I thank You that You said in Isaiah 54:4 that I am to "fear not, for [I] will not be put to shame; neither feel humiliated, for [I] will not be disgraced; but [I] will forget the shame of [my] youth."

Romans 8:1 says, "There is therefore now *no* condemnation for those who are in Christ Jesus, for the law of the Spirit of life in Christ Jesus has set you free from the law of sin and death." And if my heart has fear or condemnation, I will follow 1 John 3:19–20 when it says, "We...will assure our hearts before Him in whatever our heart condemns us; *for God is greater than our heart* and knows all things."

But even if I do sin, in 1 John 2:1–2 You said, "If anyone sins, we have an Advocate [One who will intercede for us] with the Father, Jesus Christ the righteous; and He Himself is the propitiation for our sins." Thank You, Jesus, for standing up for me before the Father!

I thank You that You said in Matthew 10:32 that "everyone who confesses Me before men, I will also confess him before My Father who is in heaven." Jesus, I confess You and all Your words to myself, my family, and the world! I am as Paul who said in Romans 1:16, "For I am not ashamed of the gospel, for it is the power of God for salvation [deliverance, healing] to everyone who believes."

Right now, I command *every spirit of shame and condemnation* to leave me in Jesus' name!

Righteousness and Acceptance

Lord, I thank You that I don't have to strive to *earn* Your love and forgiveness. You said in Titus 3:4–5, "But when the kindness of God our Savior and His love for mankind appeared, *He* saved us, not on the basis of deeds which we have done in righteousness, but according to His mercy."

And You said in Ephesians 2:8–9, "For by grace you have been saved through faith; and that not of yourselves, it is the gift of God; not as a result of works, that no one should boast." Lord, I thank You for, and now receive freely, the *gift* of salvation.

I am just as right with God the Father as Jesus is because You said in 2 Corinthians 5:21 that "He made Him [Jesus] who knew no sin to be sin on our behalf, so that we might become the righteousness of God in Him." Jesus became *my sin so* that I might become *His righteousness.* Hallelujah!

Lord, again, I thank and praise You for *accepting me* as I am *today.* I thank You that I am accepted by You *and* my brothers and sisters in the Church because You said in Ephesians 1:6, "Wherein you are accepted in the beloved" (KJV).

You said in Ephesians 2:19 that "you are no longer outsiders (exiles, migrants, and aliens, excluded from the rights of citizens), but now you share citizenship with the saints (God's own people, consecrated and set apart for Himself); and you belong to God's [own] household" (AMP).

Lord, I thank You that You said in John 15:14–16, "You are my friends...no longer do I call you slaves...but I have called you friends. You did not choose me but I chose you." Thank You for choosing me and making me Your friend. I am not Your slave or Your enemy, but a part of Your very own household.

I thank You that I do not fear any rejection that would come from You. Nor do I fear the devil's power to keep me away from You because You said in John 10:28–29, "No one shall snatch them out of My hand...and no one is able to snatch them out of My Father's hand."

I command every demon spirit of *rejection* to leave me now in Jesus' name! I am accepted and loved by God Himself, for

He has declared in John 6:29, "The one who comes to Me I will certainly not cast out."

Rejection and Love

Lord, in Hebrews 13:5–6 You said that "I will not in any way fail you nor give you up nor leave you without support. [I will] not, [I will] not, [I will] not in any degree leave you helpless nor forsake nor let [you] down, (relax My hold on you)! [Assuredly not!] So we take comfort and are encouraged and confidently and boldly say, 'The Lord is my Helper; I will not be seized with alarm [I will not fear or dread or be terrified]. What can man do to me?'" (AMP). I never need to worry that You will abandon me, for You promised that You would not, and You cannot lie.

Father, I thank You that 1 John 3:1 says, "See how great a *love* the Father has bestowed upon us, that we would be called the children of God; and such we are." I am Yours forever! You are my loving Father, not like an earthly father, but You are perfect in Your love for me. I forgive and release my earthly parents from all past judgment of their sins, faults, and rejections for I know they acted in ignorance. I love them and bless them and ask You to send Christians to preach the gospel to them.

Even King David experienced rejection, but he said in Psalm 27:10, "For my father and mother have forsaken me, but the Lord will take me up." Lord, I now know that You will take me up in Your arms and love me, embrace me, hold me tight, and never let me go.

Father God, I look to You to satisfy me and I am thankful for whatever good my earthly parents gave to me—life and the chance to live, which is something millions do not get.

You said in Leviticus 26:11, "I will make My dwelling among you, and *My soul will not reject you.*" Thank You, Lord, that You and I now live together as Father and child and that you will not reject me.

In Jeremiah 31:3, You said of me, "I have loved you with an everlasting love." I now hear You say to me, "'I have loved you,' says the Lord" (Malachi 1:2). John 15:9–10 says, *"Just as the Father has loved Me, I have also loved you*; abide in My love. If you keep My commandments, you will abide in My love."* Thank You, Jesus, that You love me the way the Father loves You! I am so thrilled that I can abide and live in Your love!

And again in Jeremiah 31:20, You say, "You are my own dear children. Don't I *love* you best of all? ...I want you to be near me, so I will have mercy on you" (CEV). Truly I can say, "The Lord is good; and His lovingkindness is everlasting" (Psalm 100:5).

I command every spirit of *fear of abandonment* and *fear of rejection* to leave me now in Jesus name!

Forgiveness and Healing

Remember, God doesn't become aware of our sin when we confess it; that is simply when we remember a proper relationship between the Forgiver and the saint, the King and the servant, the Father and the child. The point of confession is to remind us of who we are, our dependency on Him, and of His great love and mercy to forgive us. All your sins are already forgiven according to 1 John 2:1–2, but acknowledgement of this forgiveness brings healing. Just as a husband would tell his wife he is sorry for offending her, so we acknowledge our sin to the Father.

> He who conceals his transgressions will not prosper, but he who **confesses** and forsakes them **will** find compassion.
>
> —Proverbs 28:13

Say out loud:

> Father God, I come as Your child. I come before Your throne through faith in the blood of Jesus, in which I put all my trust. I come to confess and forsake my sin.

> I acknowledge my sin(s) of _____. (Be led by the Holy Spirit and don't beat yourself up. The point here is to confess specific acts that the Holy Spirit is reminding you of *now*, not things or a lifestyle that we all know needs to change over time. *He* must lead, not your old guilt and shame. If the Spirit speaks nothing, then move on.)

> Lord, I thank You that You promise to forgive me if I forgive others who have sinned against me. For You said in Mark 11:25–26, "And whenever you stand praying, forgive, if you have anything against anyone, so that your Father who is in heaven will also forgive you your transgressions. But if you do not forgive, neither will your Father who is in heaven forgive your transgressions." Again, in Luke 6:37, You said, "Pardon, and you will be pardoned." And in John 20:23, you said, "If you forgive the sins of any, their sins have been forgiven them; if you retain the sins of any, they have been retained."

> So now, according to Your command, I forgive all those who have hurt, wounded, betrayed, and sinned against me in any

way, and thus I know that You, Lord, will surely forgive me according to Your holy Word.

I agree with James 5:15–16, which says, "And the prayer offered in faith will restore the one who is sick, and the Lord will raise him up, and if he has committed sins, they will be forgiven him. Therefore, *confess* your sins to one another, and pray for one another, that you may be healed. The effective prayer of a righteous man can accomplish much."

Father, I also agree with what King David said in Psalm 32:5 that "I acknowledged my sin to You, and my iniquity I did not hide; I said 'I will *confess* my transgression to the Lord'; and you forgave the *guilt* of my sin." (Note that it says "the guilt" of your sin; guilt is the feelings of sin, the depression of it, or the sadness of what we have done. But you must let the guilt go as well as the sin itself. Let even the feelings go.)

Again, in 1 John 2:12, You said, "I am writing to you, little children, because your sins have been forgiven you for His name's sake." And Colossians 2:13 states that, "He has made you alive together with Him, having forgiven us *all* our transgressions."

Lord, I thank You that You not only *forgive* my sin, but You *forget* them, as Isaiah 38:17 says, "You have cast all my sins behind Your back." More than that, Micah 7:18–19 says, "Who is a God like You, who pardons iniquity and passes over the rebellious act of the remnant…You will cast all their sins into the depths of the sea."

Again in Psalm 86:5, You show me Your character as David prophetically declared, "For You, Lord, are good, and ready to forgive, and *abundant* in lovingkindness to *all* who call upon You."

God, I thank You that you are anxious to forgive me and have abundant mercy for my sin!

Mercy and Lovingkindness

Mercy, also translated lovingkindness, is God's unmerited favor (grace is His power or ability). It is Him extending His hand towards us, letting His countenance shine on us. It is His good actions towards us to bless us. Declare these verses out loud:

> The Lord is slow to anger and abundant in lovingkindness, forgiving iniquity and transgression. —Numbers 14:18

> O Lord, the God of Israel, there is no God like You in heaven above or on earth beneath, keeping covenant and showing **lovingkindness** to Your servants who walk before You with all their heart. —1 Kings 8:23

> O, give thanks to the Lord, for He is good; for His lovingkindness is everlasting. —1 Chronicles 16:34

> Surely goodness and lovingkindness will follow me all the days of my life. —Psalm 23:6

> All the paths of the Lord are lovingkindness and truth. —Psalm 25:10

> I will rejoice and be glad in Your lovingkindness, because You have seen my affliction; You have known the troubles of my soul. —Psalm 31:7

> My God in His lovingkindness will meet me…For You have been my stronghold. —Psalm 59:10,16

Blessed be God, Who has not turned away my prayer nor His lovingkindness from me. —Psalm 66:20

For Your lovingkindness toward me is great, and You have delivered my soul from the depths of Sheol...But You, O Lord, are a God merciful and gracious, slow to anger and abundant in lovingkindness. —Psalm 86:13,15

Fear

Say out loud:

Lord, today I also thank You that according to 2 Timothy 1:8, You said, "God has not given us a spirit of timidity, but of power and love and discipline."

I command every *spirit of fear* to leave me now in Jesus' name! (Name anything you are afraid of here and command it to go, i.e. fear of the dark, heights, death or disease, etc.)

Lord, I know You love me because 1 John 4:8 says, "God is love," and verse 18 says, "There is no fear in love [God], but perfect love [God] casts out fear."

Right now, I command every spirit of *fear of failure* to leave me in Jesus' name!

Lord, You command Joshua and all believers not to fear because You are with us. You say in Joshua 1:9, "Have not I *commanded* you? Be strong and courageous! *Do not tremble or be dismayed*, for the Lord your God is with you wherever you go."

Lord, I am so thankful that I do not have to be afraid of anything, because *You* are with *me* just as you were with Joshua! Hallelujah! Lord, you *commanded* Joshua not to be afraid and so You command me and I know that whatever You ask me to do, You will give me the *grace* to do!

I am not afraid of getting up in the morning, for Your Word says in Lamentations 3:22–23, "The Lord's lovingkindnesses indeed never cease…They are new every morning; great is Your faithfulness." Psalm 112:7 says of a godly person like me, "He will have no fear of bad news; his heart is steadfast, trusting in the Lord. His heart is secure, he will have no fear" (NIV).

So now, Lord, I do not fear what man says to me, nor do I fear whatever ungodly thoughts come to my mind, for I am fixed on trusting You. I do not even fear my own fears, but I choose this day to trust You and Your Word. I know that Your Word is true for it is by believing this Word that I was born again and baptized in the Holy Spirit, proving that this Bible is the truth. I trust it in all areas of my life, not just in a salvation to get me to heaven. The same promises by which I was born again will deliver, save, heal, strengthen, and make me whole.

I also *renounce the fear of man*, which is the reverence of man and the worship of his or her opinion of me over and above Your opinion of me, Lord. Proverbs 29:25 says, "The fear of man brings a snare, but he who *trusts* in the Lord will be exalted." Lord, I trust You and refuse to worry too much about people's opinion of me! They are not my judge and their opinion does not matter. *You* love me and that is all that matters.

Father, I thank You that I can face each day with an expectation of love and mercy and victory because each day I look to You and not to man!

Self-Pity

Father, I renounce feeling sorry for myself and repent of thoughts of self-pity. You said in Psalm 103:13 that "As a Father pitieth his children, so the Lord pitieth them that fear Him" (KJV). And again in Isaiah 63:9, You said, "In His pity He redeemed them" (KJV).

So Lord, since You have already shown me more pity than I need or deserve, I refuse to try to get more from others or myself. I will not try to manipulate others into feeling sorry for me. This is only a ploy to get attention, and You have already given me the greatest attention anyone could ask for when You died for me and then came to live in me in the Holy Spirit. I will only look to You for love and affection. I am secure in Your love for me, so I will not focus on what I don't like in life, but instead I will do as Paul wrote in Philippians 4:8 when he said, "Finally, brethren, whatever is true, whatever is honorable, whatever is right, whatever is pure, whatever is lovely, whatever is of good report, if there is any excellence and if anything worthy of praise, dwell on these things." And I will do as Colossians 3:2–3 says to "set your mind on things above, not on the things that are on earth. For you have died and your life is hidden with Christ in God." So, Lord, I set my mind now on the things of heaven. I set my mind on Your Word, for You said in Isaiah 26:3, "Thou wilt keep him in perfect peace, whose mind is stayed on thee" (KJV).

So now, Lord, my thoughts are on You, Your Word, and Your love for me all day!

Addictions

In this next section many of the verses deal with wine specifically because it was the most common chemical addiction in Bible times, but you can and should substitute any addiction you have for the word "wine" or "strong drink." Examples could include lust, masturbation, pornography, food(s), gambling, shopping, television, games and video games, gossip, and many others.

Say out loud:

> Father, I repent of all addictions in my life, including _____.
> I see that You warn me in 1 Corinthians 6:9 that "drunkards will not inherit the kingdom of God" And Galatians 5:21 says that the deeds of the flesh are "…drunkenness, carousing, and things like these, of which I forewarn you, just as I have forewarned you, that those who practice such things shall *not* inherit the kingdom of God."

> Lord, I want to inherit Your kingdom so I renounce alcohol, drunkenness, and all addictions in Jesus' name. I repent and turn away from it, for it is an idol, a false god in my life. I have looked to _____ instead of You to satisfy my soul. But you declare in Jeremiah 31:25, "For I satisfy the weary ones and refresh everyone who languishes." So, Lord, I look to You and say I am satisfied in You and not in the addiction of _____. This addiction is a lie; it fixes nothing. It promises much and delivers little.

> Lord, I see that addictions will ruin my life, and _____ deceives me. I try to escape reality with it and it will only bring me sorrow. It will bite me like a snake and poison my family and me.

> You also warn me in Proverbs 21:4 that as a king or queen (see 1 Timothy 6:15), I should not drink: "It is not for kings

to drink wine, or for rulers to desire strong drink." Hosea 4:11–12 says, "Harlotry, wine and new wine take away the understanding…for a spirit of harlotry has led them astray." To get drunk is to be whore against You. Alcohol and any addiction is an idol.

You also compare drinkers of wine with dogs in Isaiah 56:10–12, saying, "All of them are mute dogs unable to bark, dreamers lying down, who love to slumber; and the dogs are greedy, they are not satisfied…. 'Come,' they say, 'let us get wine, and let us drink heavily of strong drink; and tomorrow will be like today, only more so.'"

You also say in Isaiah 5:22, 24, "Woe to those who are heroes at drinking wine...their root will become like rot and their blossom blow away as dust; for they have rejected the law of the Lord."

Father, in light of all these warnings, how can I continue to _____? If I do this, it is because I am a slave to sin and the spirits of lust, rebellion, and addiction. I ask You, Jesus, to set me free. You declared in John 8:34–35 that "everyone who commits sin is the slave of sin," *but*, "if the Son makes you free, you will be free indeed." I ask you to set me free now in Jesus' name!

I fall out of agreement with the demon spirits of addiction and abuse, the curse of alcoholism, and the curse of pride, idolatry, harlotry, and rebellion now in Jesus' name. I command these spirits to leave me now and go to the pit, never to return to me again!

Lord, I ask You to change my heart. Give me a hatred for this sin of idolatry and drunkenness and all the sins of the flesh. Lord, I cry out to You for mercy and the grace to change.

As I do this, I confess that I hate all addictions. I hate it because You hate it, Lord, and I turn away from it today. I renounce addiction now in Jesus' name. I renounce rebellion and harlotry now in Jesus' name! I fall out of agreement with these spirits and close the doors of my sin in this area and I close the spiritual doors of my father's sins to the thousandth generation.

For Other Issues

For a problem you're facing that is not covered in these confessions, use an online Bible website like www.biblegateway.com or a physical concordance to look up key words for verses that will help you. You must be able to speak or quote scriptures that apply to your problem area. You will want to buy the same concordance as the Bible translation you mostly use. NASB corresponds to Holman's Exhaustive Concordance, KJV and NKJV correspond to Strong's Exhaustive Concordance.

For example, if all you know is that you're struggling with a curse of some kind, you would find through your search an applicable scripture for "curse," which is Galatians 3:13. You could then pray, "Today in Jesus' name, I renounce all curses of fear, rejection, religion, condemnation, pride, alcoholism, lust, rebellion and witchcraft. According to Galatians 3:13, "Christ redeemed us from the curse of the Law, having become a curse for us—for it is written, 'Cursed is everyone who hangs on a tree.'"

I encourage you to make your own confession sheet so it will be pertinent to your struggles and temptations. After you type them out, be sure to say them to yourself on a *regular* basis. The spirit of rejection trained you for many years and you thus have an inner image of yourself that needs to be renewed (see Romans 12:1–2). This takes time and is a vital part of your deliverance.

He Who Has Begun a Good Work in You...

No matter where you find yourself today, I am confident of these words from Philippians 1:6:

> He who began a good work in you will perfect it until the day of Christ Jesus.

Pray this final prayer with me:

> Yes, Lord. I say "Amen!" to this promise. You have begun a good work and You will perfect it in me until the day of Christ Jesus. According to Hebrews 13:21, I declare that You are my great Shepherd through the blood of the eternal covenant. Thank you that you are equipping me in every good thing to do Your will, working in me that which is pleasing in Your sight, through Jesus Christ, to whom be the glory forever and ever.
>
> Romans 8:37 proclaims the truth that I am more than a conqueror through Jesus Christ who loves me. I will overcome all rejection and receive the perfect love You have for me. According to 2 Timothy 4:7–8, I will fight the good fight, I will finish the course, and I will keep the faith for You have laid up for me a crown of righteousness, which You will award to me on that day when my race is completed. Until then, come abide in me and I in You as You lead me in Your paths of righteousness for Your name's sake. Amen!

ENDNOTES

1. By permission. From *Merriam-Webster's Collegiate Dictionary*, 11th Edition ©2012 by Merriam-Webster, Incorporated (www.merriam-webster.com).

2. Jacqueline L. Salmon, "Most Americans Believe in Higher Power, Poll Finds." Washington Post. Tuesday, June 24, 2008. http://www.washingtonpost.com/wp-dyn/content/story/2008/06/23/ST2008062300818.html.

3. CNN, "Jackson rabbi-friend: Singer was 'a tortured, tortured soul.'" June 30, 2012. http://edition.cnn.com/2009/SHOWBIZ/Music/06/30/jackson.rabbi/index.html.

4. Wayne Jacobsen, *He Loves Me!* (Newbury Park, CA: Windblown Media, 2007).

5. Ibid.

6. *American Heritage Dictionary*. Copyright 2011 Houghton Mifflin Harcourt Publishing Company. All rights reserved. http://ahdictionary.com.

7. Ibid.

www.northfirenet.com